THE IRISH
IN THE AMERICAN
CIVIL WAR

THE IRISH
IN THE AMERICAN
CIVIL WAR

DAMIAN SHIELS

First published 2013
Reprinted 2014, 2019, 2022

The History Press
97 St George's Place,
Cheltenham, GL50 3QB
www.thehistorypress.co.uk

British Library Cataloguing in Publication Data.
A catalogue record for this book is available from the British Library.

ISBN 978 1 84588 768 1

Typesetting and origination by The History Press
Printed and bound by TJ Books Limited, Padstow, Cornwall

Contents

Acknowledgements

The origins of this book lie with a decision I took in May 2010 to establish a site dedicated to telling people in Ireland about a remarkable generation of Irish emigrants (www.irishamericancivilwar.com).

The book has benefited greatly from the superb resource that is the Library of Congress Prints & Photographs Collection. My good friend and colleague Brian MacDomhnaill kindly took the opportunity on a recent visit to the US to take a few key photographs on my behalf, for which I am extremely grateful. I am equally indebted to Joe Maghe, who kindly granted permission for the use of some of the images from his most remarkable collection. Thanks also to friend James B. Swan, author of *Chicago's Irish Legion*, for sharing information on his research regarding the 90th Illinois Infantry. I am grateful to Ian Kenneally for taking the time to read and comment on the 'Recruiting for the Irish Brigade' chapter and his advice generally.

The first book I owned on the American Civil War was a day-by-day account of the conflict, and was the kernel of an interest that has grown considerably over the past twenty years. I am grateful to Vincent Shiels for sparking that interest.

I would never have reached this stage without the constant encouragement, support and advice of Angela Gallagher, who also kindly read and commented on a draft of this book. She deserves enormous credit for helping me along the way. Similarly Sara Nylund has provided me with invaluable support and encouragement throughout my career. She has also used her extensive artistic abilities to improve many of my papers and articles, including an example in this work. It is to Angela and Sara that this book is dedicated.

Introduction

The American Civil War is Ireland's great forgotten conflict. In 1860 no fewer than 1.6 million Irish people lived in the United States. This does not include many of the first-generation members of the Irish-American community who had been born following their family's emigration across the Atlantic. During the American Civil War itself some 150,000 Irish fought for the Union, with at least another 20,000 in the service of the Confederacy. Although there are no figures for the number of Irish who died, it most certainly ran to thousands. Unfortunately the experiences of this huge number of Irish people, the majority of whom were Famine emigrants, remains little understood in Ireland.[1]

Today the chief interest in the Irish experience of the American Civil War rests in the United States, where it remains a topic of fascination for many, particularly those of Irish descent. Few books are published in Ireland on the Irish experience of the war, there are few memorials, and its impact is rarely discussed. Those Irish who fought in the Civil War who are remembered tend to be those who have connections to Fenianism or Irish nationalism. In Ireland the American Civil War is generally regarded as just another conflict in which Irish soldiers fought, an extension of the 'Wild Geese' tradition, to be compared with Irish contributions to the armies of Spain and France in the sixteenth, seventeenth and eighteenth centuries. But the conflagration that erupted in America in 1861 was very different. It had a much larger impact on Irish people, impacts that were felt by an entire community.

At first glance, given the fact that the Great Famine is regarded as a defining moment in Irish history, it seems incongruous that the subsequent traumatic experience of so many of its victims does not receive greater attention in Ireland. The Famine is rightfully remembered here, as is the physical fact that vast numbers of people were forced to leave the country as a result. However, Ireland largely leaves the memory of these emigrants at the dockside, as they boarded ships to a new life far from home. Despite the broader pride that Ireland takes in her global diaspora, examining and remembering the experiences of emigrants once they arrived in their new countries has been largely left to their descendants in those countries, a role they continue to fulfil.

The remembrance of the American Civil War sits in stark contrast to the only other Irish experience of conflict that compares with it – the First World War. The Great War has been described as 'proportionately the greatest deployment of armed manpower in the history of Irish militarism'. In the region of 200,000 Irishmen fought in the 1914–18 conflict, and some 35,000 lost their lives. These are strikingly similar figures to those for the Irish in the American Civil War. The service of Irishmen in the First World War has undergone a welcome rehabilitation in Ireland over the last fifteen years or so. Long neglected, the Irish experience of the First World War has now spawned a proliferation of books, the rebirth of regimental organisations and associations and the regular attention of the regional and national media. How then can it be that the similarly scaled American Civil War, which affected over a million and a half Irish people, remains largely unrecognised in Ireland?[2]

There are a number of probable reasons for this differential memory. The First World War is fifty years closer to us in history, and has become a major focus of commemoration across Europe, as the last veterans have recently passed away and the centennial fast approaches. Whereas the Irish soldiers who went to fight in the First World War left Ireland, and, if they survived, returned here, those who fought in the American Civil War were physically removed from the island, and few returned after the war's conclusion. Perhaps the major reason is the direct connection that many Irish people feel to the First World War. A large number of the current population can trace their family back to a direct antecedent who experienced life in the trenches. Interest in a major historic event naturally grows when viewed through the prism of an ancestor's life. That link was broken for the Irish emigrants of the nineteenth century – their descendants grew up in the United States, not Ireland. The finality of their departure has been accentuated; with the passage of time the Irish who lived in the America of 1860 have become more divorced from their homeland, and ultimately interest in their experiences has faded in the land of their birth.

This book is an attempt to raise awareness in Ireland of some of the remarkable and poignant stories that relate to the Irish in the American Civil War. It is particularly relevant at a time when the 150th anniversary of the Civil War is ongoing. The chapters that follow do not present a narrative history of Irish involvement in the war, and are not intended to provide the reader with a comprehensive knowledge of all things Irish in that conflict. Rather each chapter is in the form of an individual story, selected to provide a flavour of the wide-ranging and varied experiences of Irish men, women and children before, during and after the guns started firing. Through these stories some of the major themes that had a bearing on the Irish community in America at the time are explored. Wars are not just a matter of battles and sieges, victory and defeat. Violent actions have a ripple effect, with often devastating consequences that reach beyond the immediacy of combat. To gain a fuller picture of these effects it is not enough to look just at the experience of Irish soldiers in battle, although this remains important. A wider view has to be taken to reveal the true scale and true cost of war. The conflict that occurred in America between 1861 and 1865 had the scale and extracted a cost on the Irish community in the United States that is worthy of remembrance.

The stories have been arranged under four major themes, each covering an aspect of the Irish experience. In 'Beginnings', the stories concentrate on the pre-war years and the start of the conflict, as many Irishmen had front row seats to the making of history. 'Realities' examines the war in further detail, charting the stories of some Irish soldiers as they came face-to-face with industrialised warfare and its result. In 'The Wider War' some of the other facets of the conflict are explored, particularly the experiences of Irish women and non-combatants at the front, as well as the war of subterfuge that went on in Ireland. The final theme, 'Aftermath', is a study of the consequences of the American Civil War, and how it continued to affect countless Irish veterans and their families until well into the twentieth century. Above all, it is hoped that these stories will spark further interest in the topic on the part of the reader – if so, it will have achieved its aim.

A note on conventions

The accounts in this book are largely drawn from contemporary documents. Punctuation and spelling were often more haphazard in the nineteenth century, and some of the accounts use language in a form that appears unfamiliar to us today. To maintain the integrity of the primary accounts they have been reproduced as they first appeared. This includes the American spelling of English words, which in the remainder of the text follows the European style. The only exception to this is when referring to military terminology, so for example 'colors' is preferred to 'colours.'

Beginnings

The Irish played a part in United States history long before the outbreak of the American Civil War. Some held prominent positions in professions such as the law or politics; almost twenty years before the Civil War, one Irish politician found himself in a position where he could have had a profound influence on the future of the United States and the man who was to become the sixteenth President. However, the majority of Irish people remained on the lower rungs of the social ladder, and were content to carve out a livelihood as best they could. Long before 1861 service in the army and navy was a particular draw for those born in Ireland, and as a result almost every major military incident leading up to the war was witnessed by Irish soldiers or sailors. The same was true when the war started at Fort Sumter, South Carolina, when Irish soldiers in the Federal garrison outnumbered all other nationalities, including American.

As the war began to escalate, Abraham Lincoln called for volunteers to suppress the rebellion. This ultimately led to the first battle of the war, when two inexperienced and naïve armies met on 21 July 1861 at the First Battle of Bull Run, Virginia. Irish fought on both sides of this engagement, which ended in Confederate victory. For some it would be their first and their last battle. Bull Run set the tone for what would be a long war. There was a need for more men and more regiments, and so recruitment continued apace. The leaders of the Irish community, eager to play their part in the conflict, had to find ways to persuade their countrymen to enlist, particularly given the severe discrimination many had received from some sections of American society in previous years. Ultimately many did volunteer, the majority in non-Irish units but some also in ethnic Irish companies and regiments, which marched to war beneath green banners. In their ranks went men from every county on the island of Ireland.

The duel that almost changed history

The past is filled with 'what if' moments – those occasions where a slightly different sequence of events may have radically altered history as we know it. One such incident occurred on 22 September 1842, when James Shields prepared to meet a fellow Illinois politician in a duel. Although the American Civil War was twenty years in the future, decisions that Shields made that day had the potential to radically alter the story of his adopted country. The man he was preparing to meet had been born in Kentucky but was now practising law in Illinois. Notable for his unusual height, he had started to make an impression in the world of politics – his name was Abraham Lincoln, future President of the United States.

By 1842 James Shields was already a well-known figure in Illinois. He was born around 10 May 1810 in Altmore, Co. Tyrone, and had settled in

Kaskaskia, Illinois by 1826. While in Ireland he had been well-educated, and unlike many of his Irish contemporaries James was well-placed for social advancement. He soon got involved in the practice of law and politics, and was elected as a Democrat to the Illinois Legislature, beginning his service in 1836. His political career began to take-off, and Shields became the State Auditor, responsible for Illinois's funds. It was while holding this office for a second-term that the sequence of events which led to the Lincoln duel took place.[3]

In the early 1840s the United States was in the midst of a depression caused by the 'Panic of 1837', a financial crisis which had swept across the country and led to years of economic difficulty. In 1842 the situation in Illinois had deteriorated to such an extent that Shields did not trust the value of the paper money in the state – as a result he and others in the Democratic Party felt it necessary to direct that Illinois's taxes be collected in gold and silver only. Abraham Lincoln, at this time a member of the Whig Party, was strongly opposed to the policy, particularly as it meant the State was going to refuse to accept its own paper money.[4]

Lincoln determined to speak out against Shields and the Democrats, and began his campaign with the publication of an anonymous satirical letter in Springfield's *Sangamo Journal*. In his piece, dated 27 August 1842 and entitled 'A Letter from the Lost Township', Lincoln took the fictional role of a widow called 'Rebecca', who was horrified to learn that State Bank paper would no longer be accepted as payment for taxes. 'Rebecca' cast aspersions on Shields and his fellow officials, implying their principal concern was maintaining the value of their own income rather than helping the people of the State. Shields was referred to as a 'fool and a liar' and accused of making a 'dunce' of himself with women. If matters had ended here the prospect of a confrontation between the two men may not have arisen. However, Lincoln had shown the letter to his friends Julia Jayne and soon to be wife Mary Todd, and both women found its content extremely humorous. They decided they would aid Lincoln by writing their own anonymous satirical letters deriding Shields in the press. The women also chose 'Rebecca' as their central character, and took aim at the Irishman's supposed outrage at the initial published piece. This time 'Rebecca' spoke of how Shields was 'mad as a march hare' about the original letter, and that in recompense for her offence the fictional widow would allow Shields to come and 'squeeze her hand'. The ladies' contribution ended with an offer of marriage by 'Rebecca' to Shields, together with a poem describing her union with 'Erin's Son'.[5]

The follow up publications were the final straw for the now ridiculed Shields, who determined to find out who had written them so he could demand a retraction. He contacted the editor of the *Journal* to learn who had conjured up 'Rebecca'. Lincoln, keen to protect the two women's integrity, took full responsibility for all the letters. With the supposed true identity of 'Rebecca' revealed, the incensed Irishman wrote to the future President on 17 September:

> … In two or three of the last numbers of the Sangamo Journal, articles of the most personal nature and calculated to degrade me, have made their appearance. On enquiring I was informed by the editor of that paper, through the medium of my friend, Gen. Whiteside, that you are the author of these articles. This information satisfies me that I have become by some means or other, the object of your secret hostility. I will not take the trouble of enquiring into the reason of all this, but I will take the liberty of requiring a full, positive and absolute retraction of all offensive allusions used by you in these communications, in relation to my private character and standing as a man, as an apology for the insults conveyed in them. This may prevent consequences which no one will regret more than myself.[6]

Lincoln responded by stating that Shields had rushed to the accusation without checking all his facts, and somewhat disingenuously added that he had not specified what he had found offensive in the letters content. He refused to respond to Shields' demands because of what he perceived as the 'menace' in the tone of the note. Both men's blood was now up, and neither was in a mood to back down. As the situation escalated, Shields wrote again to Lincoln, asking if he was the author of the letters as the editor of the *Journal* had stated, and saying that it was 'not my intention to menace, but to do myself justice'. Again, Lincoln refused to discuss the matter further unless Shields retracted the first note, which he considered offensive. The Irishman's response was to demand the satisfaction of a duel. Shields appointed John D. Whiteside as his second, while Lincoln appointed Elias H. Merryman – the stage was now set for a bloody confrontation.[7]

As Lincoln had been challenged it was his prerogative to determine the details of the encounter. He entered into considerable detail on this point, writing down the exact specifications for Merryman to follow. Lincoln decided that the weapon of choice would be large cavalry broadswords of equal size and identical in all respects. He even recommended they be similar to those then being used by a cavalry company in Jacksonville. In addition he specified that a 10ft long plank of 9 to 12ins thickness should be placed on edge between him and Shields, across which neither should cross upon pain of death. The duelling area was to be a line drawn on the ground on either side of the plank and parallel to it, at a distance of a sword-length plus 3ft – to cross this line would be an indication of surrender. There was method to Lincoln's choice of weapon and specifications for the fight. While Shields was 5ft 9ins, Lincoln towered above him at 6ft 4ins. The Kentuckian hoped to use his superior reach to his advantage, and intended to disarm the Irishman with his weapon; he had previously trained for a month in its use and felt comfortable wielding it. Lincoln would later cite another reason for his selection of swords: 'I didn't want the darned fellow to kill me, which I rather think he would have done if we had selected pistols.'[8]

James Shields, who challenged Abraham Lincoln to a duel in 1842. (Library of Congress)

Abraham Lincoln in the 1840s. (Library of Congress)

With the format decided, the rival parties still had a major obstacle to overcome in order to see the affair through. Duelling was illegal in Illinois, and so it was necessary to travel beyond the state to prevent both men from violating the law and being prosecuted. Rumours that affidavits were being drawn up for the men's arrest sped them on their way. Both Lincoln and Shields made for Alton on the Mississippi River, from where they would take a boat to Missouri and the suitably named Bloody Island. With this final detail determined, the Shields–Lincoln duel was scheduled for Thursday 22 September 1842 at 5 p.m.[9]

Each of the rivals brought three associates to bear witness to events. Their companions had attempted to bring about an amicable settlement, but now that they had arrived in Missouri it seemed little could prevent the confrontation. As the hour of the duel neared John J. Hardin and R.W. English, mutual friends of both Lincoln and Shields, were speeding after the duelling parties. They had been horrified to learn of the potentially violent conclusion to the dispute, and determined to prevent it. Arriving just in time, they asked both men to consider appointing a panel of four or five of their friends to adjudicate on the matter. Both sides agreed to enter discussions, and with the crisis temporarily averted, the Shields party asked the Lincoln party to explain the publication of the letters. At this juncture there was no longer any advantage in Lincoln protecting the two ladies by claiming he had written all the letters and so his party stated that Lincoln had in fact only written the first letter, and that he had no intention of injuring the personal or private character of the Irishman. Although the men accompanying him were willing to accept this explanation, it was some time before the fiery Shields acceded and the dispute was ended. Abraham Lincoln was able to return to Illinois and continue his political advancement, which eighteen years later would see him become President of the United States.[10]

James Shields' career did not suffer as a result of his scrape with Lincoln, and indeed both men became friends in later years. The Tyrone man would go on to become a justice of the State Supreme Court and serve as a commissioner of the land office in Washington. He achieved further notoriety during the 1846-8 war with Mexico, when he served as Brigadier-General of Illinois Volunteers and was seriously wounded at the Battle of Cerro Gordo. While leading a charge against the enemy the

Irishman was struck by grapeshot, which passed through his right lung and exited near the spine. At the time the wound was thought mortal, but Shields survived and his actions sealed his martial reputation. The Irishman was brevetted a major-general and commended by his commanding officer Winfield Scott. Shields next served as senator for Illinois from 1849-55, before moving to Minnesota where he was also elected to the Senate on behalf of that state.[11]

The outbreak of the American Civil War found the Irishman in California, but he soon travelled east to take up a position as Brigadier-General of United States Volunteers, being commissioned on 19 August 1861. Although he was initially mentioned for command of the Irish Brigade, he declined the offer, hoping to be given control of a larger force. His expectations were met when he was placed at the head of a division, but unfortunately for Shields his Civil War performance was not destined to emulate that of the Mexican campaign. In 1862 the Irishman and his division were positioned in the Shenandoah Valley, Virginia, where they came up against one of the Confederacy's most famous Generals, Thomas J. 'Stonewall' Jackson. Their initial encounter was at the Battle of Kernstown, where on 23 March 1862 Shields' force inflicted the only defeat Jackson suffered in his career. Although quick to claim the victory for himself in the national press, Shields had in fact been incapacitated at the time of the engagement and in reality had contributed little to the outcome. His subsequent erratic performance in the handling of his men began to raise questions about his abilities, and his fate was sealed when much of his force was defeated by Jackson at the Battle of Port Republic on 9 June. He was never given another field command, and he resigned from the army on 28 March 1863. Despite the setback of his Civil War career Shields would re-enter political life, and in 1879 he was selected to fill an unexpired Senate seat in Missouri. With this Shields became the only person in United States history to have served as a Senator for three separate states. The Tyrone man did not seek re-election on the expiration of his term due to poor health, and instead embarked on a lecture tour. It was during this trip that he fell ill in Ottumwa, Iowa, where he died on 1 June 1879. He is buried in St Mary's Cemetery, Carrollton, Missouri.[12]

James Shields had made a success of his time in the United States. He carved out an impressive political career, although his failings during the Civil War tarnished his military reputation. However, the most intriguing aspect of the proud and forthright man's life must remain his near duel with the future President in 1842, one of the great 'what if' moments in American history.

Witness to the first shots

The history of the Irish in the American Civil War has tended to focus only on those who served in the army, be they famous Generals such as Patrick Ronayne Cleburne or famous units like the Irish Brigade. However, the Irish also numbered in their thousands in the naval service, particularly among the Union Navy. Perhaps the most notable was Dubliner Stephen Clegg Rowan, who would go on to become a Vice-Admiral in the United States navy, and have no fewer than four ships named in his honour. The Irishman could also make a claim that few others could match – he had been there when it all began, as Confederate shells began to rain down on Fort Sumter, South Carolina on 12 April 1861.

Stephen Rowan was born in Dublin on Christmas Day 1808, but was still a child when he emigrated with his father to Pennsylvania. They later settled in Piqua, Ohio where the young Stephen worked as a store clerk before enrolling in the state's Miami University in 1825. He became a Midshipman in the navy the following year, beginning a military career that would span over sixty years. It was 1846 before Rowan, now a lieutenant, gained his first combat experience in the war with Mexico. He acquitted himself well, participating in a number of expeditions including the capture of Los Angeles. The year 1861 found the now vastly experienced naval man in command of the sloop-of-war the USS *Pawnee*. On 4 April that year the Irish Commander was in Washington when he received the following telegram from Secretary of the Navy, Gideon Welles:

> Sir, You will proceed immediately with the U.S. Steam sloop Pawnee to the navy yard at Norfolk, for the purpose of receiving a month's supply of provisions. The commandant of the yard there will be directed to have them ready to be put on board immediately on her arrival.

The directive had come straight from President Abraham Lincoln – whether Rowan knew it or not, he had been set on a path that would lead to him witnessing one of the most momentous events in American history.[13]

The crisis to which the Dubliner had been ordered to respond had been brewing since the end of 1860. On 20 December that year South Carolina had become the first Southern state to secede from the Union. At the time Major Robert Anderson was in command of a small force based at Fort Moultrie in South Carolina's Charleston Harbor. Suddenly finding himself in what for all intents and purposes was enemy territory, Anderson decided to move his men to the more secure Fort Sumter, which lay in the middle of the harbor. Here he effectively became besieged, and as the months passed and food supplies dwindled Anderson's situation became increasingly desperate. Abraham Lincoln had been in office for less than a month (he was inaugurated on 4 March 1861) when he had to make a decision about Fort Sumter's future – a decision he knew could have long-lasting ramifications. His choices were either to allow the position to run out of supplies and fall into the hands of the Southerners, or to attempt to resupply the beleaguered garrison. He decided on the latter course.

When Rowan was ordered to proceed to Norfolk he had no details as to his mission. He received a further communication on 5 April from Gideon Welles:

> Sir, After the Pawnee shall have been provisioned at Norfolk you will proceed with her to sea and on the morning of the 11th instant appear off Charleston bar, 10 miles distant from and due east of the light-house, where you will report to Captain Samuel Mercer, of the Powhatan, for special service. Should he not be there, you will await his arrival.

Although he had not been informed as to the specifics of his task, the Irishman must have suspected it had something to do with Fort Sumter. Having loaded his provisions on board at Norfolk, Stephen Rowan and the Pawnee headed south.[14]

Rowan's ship was not the only one making its way towards Fort Sumter. Other members of the flotilla included the civilian steamer *Baltic*, which carried supplies and 200 reinforcements for the fort; the USS *Harriet Lane* and USS *Pocahontas*, and the tugs *Freeborn*, *Yankee* and *Uncle Ben*. A strong easterly gale struck the *Pawnee* after she left Norfolk, seriously hampering her progress. By 10 April Rowan had only travelled as far as Cape Henry, Virginia, and it would be a further two days before the *Pawnee* arrived at her destination.[15]

On the morning of 12 April 1861 Rowan and the *Pawnee* arrived at their designated position of Charleston Harbor. A small paddle steamer approached the ship, which proved to be the *Harriet Lane*. A boat from the steamer approached the *Pawnee* and Rowan was handed an order dated 5 April. The fateful communication outlined just what was expected of the Irishman and his crew; the seriousness of the situation that faced them must have been immediately apparent to all concerned. The order that Rowan read was from Secretary Welles to Captain Samuel Mercer of the *Powhatan*:

> ... The primary object of the expedition is to provision Fort Sumter, for which purpose the War Department will furnish the necessary transports. Should the authorities at Charleston permit the fort to be supplied, no further particular service will be required of the force under your command ... Should the authorities at Charleston, however, refuse to permit or attempt to prevent the vessel or vessels having supplies on board from entering the harbor or from peaceably proceeding to Fort Sumter, you will protect the transports or boats of the expedition in the object of their mission, disposing of your force in such a manner as to open the way for ingress, and afford, as far as practicable, security to the men and boats, and repelling by force, if necessary, all obstructions towards provisioning the fort and reinforcing it; for in case of resistance to the peaceable primary object of the expedition a reinforcement of the garrison will also be attempted.[16]

The implications of the order were clear – if resistance was encountered it was to be responded to in kind. Any firing on the fort or the naval vessels during the resupply attempt would be seen as an act of war.

Captain Fox of the *Baltic* was the man charged with coordinating the resupply efforts, and he was next aboard the *Pawnee* to discuss the situation with Rowan. As the *Pawnee* and the other main vessels were too large to pass into the harbor, Fox had devised a strategy whereby the three tugs would approach Fort Sumter with the men and supplies. In order to aid these efforts Rowan had a launch and cutter armed and readied to accompany the tugs. As the minutes passed, the *Harriet Lane* and the *Baltic* stood in towards the bar to commence the operation. However, before much time had elapsed the *Baltic* came out again and approached the *Pawnee*. Captain Fox brought shocking news – the forts and batteries around the harbor had started to fire on Fort Sumter. Commander

Rowan, with Fox still on board, moved the *Pawnee* in to have a closer look. He saw fire directed at Sumter from Fort Moultrie, Cumming's Point, Fort Johnson and the harbor's sand and floating batteries. Major Anderson and his small garrison were returning fire as best they could. The Southern forces had decided to start firing on the fort to force its surrender before Rowan and his comrades could resupply them.[17]

Captain Fox decided he would attempt to resupply the Fort again the following morning with protection from Rowan. However, the *Baltic* ran aground on Rattlesnake Shoal, further delaying relief attempts until the night of 13 April. While waiting for the *Baltic* to free herself the *Pawnee* spotted a schooner passing close by, and suspecting it might belong to the forces in Charleston, Commander Rowan decided to give chase. The ship was brought to anchor after a number of shots were fired across her bows, but she proved to be a vessel from Philadelphia carrying ice. The Irishman decided to commandeer the trader for the transfer of men and provisions, but events were destined to overtake his plans. He described what happened next:

> This arrangement had scarcely been determined upon before a dense smoke issued from the weather side of Fort Sumter; for some time it was thought to be some floating fire craft dropped down against the walls to annoy and prevent the accuracy of Major Anderson's fire. In two hours flames appeared above the ramparts on the opposite side of the fort from our position. At noon, or a little later, a body of flames curled far above the ramparts. We then became satisfied that the fort was on fire and feared that the gallant major and his little band would suffer severely … At about 2 o'clock the flagstaff on Fort Sumter was shot away, as we witnessed the sad spectacle of the fall of our flag, which we were so impotent to assist. In vain we looked for its reappearance over the fort; instead of this, the firing

from Sumter became more and more weak, and at length ceased entirely.[18]

A boat was taken by Lieutenant Marcy under a flag of truce to the enemy position at Cumming's Point to determine if the fort had surrendered. Marcy returned with the news that it had. As part of the surrender terms the garrison of Sumter was allowed to depart with the ships. All that was left for Commander Rowan and the *Pawnee* to do was assist in their transfer to the *Baltic*, and on 15 April he and the others set off for home.

The events that the Dubliner witnessed in Charleston Harbor proved to be the first shots of the American Civil War. With the firing on Fort Sumter a conflict had been brought about which would drag on for four bloody years, costing in the region of 750,000 lives. The events that Rowan participated in that April can truly be described as some of the momentous and far-reaching in American history.[19]

Stephen Rowan went on to perform well during the war, perhaps most notably in command of the naval contingent at New Bern during the Burnside Expedition. He would rise from the rank of Commander in 1861 to Commodore by war's end. Along the way he commanded well-known vessels such as the *Brooklyn*, *Powhatan* and *New Ironsides*. His service continued after the conclusion of the Civil War; in 1866 he became a Rear-Admiral and would eventually rise to Vice-Admiral. In post-war years he variously served as Commandant of Norfolk Navy Yard, commander of the US Asiatic Squadron, Commandant of the New York Navy Yard and Governor of the Naval Asylum. Rowan retired from active service in April 1889, having amassed over sixty years in the service of the United States Navy.

He died in Washington DC on 31 March 1890 where he is buried with his wife in Oak Hill Cemetery. Throughout his long career this little-known Irishman surely experienced few days that compared with 12 April 1861. One wonders if he realised then that he was witnessing the start of such a horrific and hard-fought conflict. Whatever his thoughts

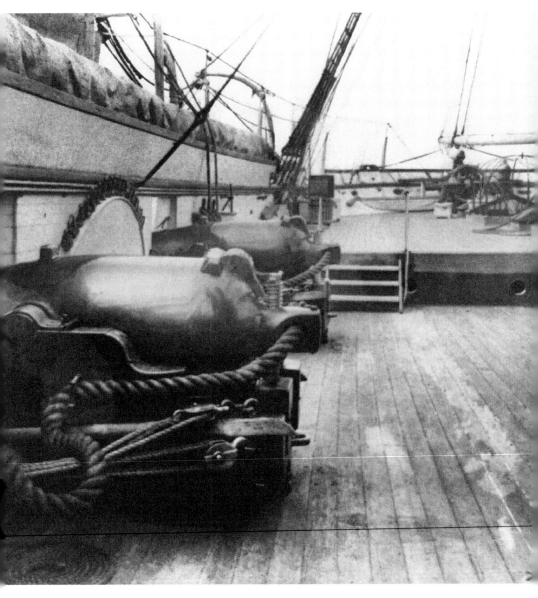

The deck of the USS *Pawnee* as it appeared in 1861. (Library of Congress)

at the time, what is certain was that he was one of the very few Union men who was there to see it all begin.[20]

The Irish at Sumter

Even before the American Civil War erupted in 1861, thousands of Irishmen were already serving in the United States military, as part of the regular army. Attracted by the offer of steady pay and board, as well as a means of escaping the slum-like conditions that were the lot of the urban poor, a soldierly life proved a popular choice for immigrants of the 1840s and '50s. Of the 3,516 foreign-born men who entered the US Army between 1850 and 1851, 2,113 of them were Irish. There was such an influx of Irishmen into the service that during the 1850s almost 60 per cent of the entire army came from Ireland. Of the 16,000 men who constituted the US Army in 1860, thousands had been born on the other side of the Atlantic.[21]

As the United States slid inexorably towards war in the years before 1861, one incident stood out as an event that polarised Northern and Southern opinion. A militant abolitionist called John Brown decided that he would attempt to start an armed slave uprising against the South. In order to achieve this he targeted the United States Arsenal at Harper's Ferry, Virginia (now West Virginia) which he planned to capture before distributing weapons to the insurrectionists. To this end he led eighteen men towards the town on the night of 16 October 1859, but his plan misfired when the alarm was raised, and slaves failed to join the revolt. By 17 October locals were beginning to take pot shots at the party, and a number of the raiders and townspeople were killed. With escape cut off, Brown led his survivors and prisoners into the arsenal's fire-engine house to make a last stand.

Eventually a detachment of US Marines were rushed to the scene, and placed under the temporary command of Colonel Robert E. Lee of the

2nd US Cavalry (Lee would later lead the Army of Northern Virginia). Although not attached to the army, the marines also had a large number of Irishmen in their ranks. Brown refused to surrender, and the marines were ordered to storm the fire-engine house. With a battering ram and bayonets the troops surged forward, breaking in and killing two of Brown's men. John Brown himself was taken alive. The action divided North and South as never before. Southerners, terrified at the prospect of slave revolt, ensured that the abolitionist (along with six others) was swiftly tried and hanged. In the North, Brown became a martyr, and the desire for an end to slavery gained more purchase in many of the Free states.

US Marines storming the Engine House at Harper's Ferry, Virginia, in 1859, the attack in which Private Luke Quinn died. (Library of Congress)

The Confederate bombardment of Fort Sumter in April 1861. (Library of Congress)

The attack on the fire-engine house at Harper's Ferry had cost the marines one fatality, twenty-four-year-old Irishman Private Luke Quinn. He had enlisted in Brooklyn, New York nearly four years earlier, on 23 November 1855. During the assault, Luke had been the third man to scramble through the shattered door and into the building, where he was instantly shot in the abdomen, dying a few minutes later. The prominence of an Irishman as the only military fatality of John Brown's raid established a pattern that would be repeated less than two years later, as the first shots of the Civil War were aimed at Fort Sumter.[22]

It was around 4.30 a.m. on 12 April 1861 when Confederate artillery opened fire on Fort Sumter in Charleston Harbor, South Carolina. These shots marked the start of the American Civil War. Inside the fort were forty civilian workers, a civilian clerk, an African-American servant and eighty-six officers and enlisted men under the command of Major Robert Anderson. Of the eighty-six soldiers, only twenty-three had been born in the United States. No fewer than thirty-eight were Irish, making up 63 per cent of the foreign-born and almost 44 per cent of all soldiers who endured that first Confederate fire of the war.[23]

In the months that preceded the firing on Sumter the nation had been gripped by the siege of the fort, as everyone wondered what the outcome of the stand-off would be. On 7 January 1861 the *New York Times* was able to report that, for the first time, they were able to bring their readers the thoughts of one of the soldiers besieged in Charleston Harbor. They were referring to a letter originally published by the *Rochester Democrat*, which had been written by Private James Gibbons of Company E, 1st US Artillery. Gibbons was one of the Irish members of the garrison, having been born in Co. Galway around 1833. He had penned the letter to his wife on 29 December 1860, only three days after the men had moved into Fort Sumter from Fort Moultrie. The *New York Times* reported it as follows:

> He [Gibbons] writes under the date of Dec. 29, gives a brief account of the withdrawal of the little army of Major Anderson from Fort Moultrie on the night of the 23d of December [sic], and says, "We set the fort on fire, and cut down the flag-staff before we left." He also states that 300 men from Charleston came the next day and occupied Fort Moultrie. This soldier is supposed to breadth the spirit that prevails in Fort Sumter, for he says "we are ready to fight, and intend to clean 'em out." Such a letter from an honest soldier in the fort, addressed to his wife, is of more

value as indicating the state of affairs there than telegraphic dispatches sent from Charleston from secession sources. This is the first that we have heard of the feeling of the soldiers at Fort Sumter since that position was occupied by Maj. Anderson's party.[24]

James Gibbons was a typical career Irish soldier in the pre-war US Army. Most likely a Famine emigrant, by 1861 he was already a ten-year veteran, having enlisted in Rochester, New York, on 14 November 1851. The then labourer was described as 5ft 7¾ins in height, with grey eyes, brown hair and a fair complexion. Like many other Irishmen in the regular service, he had seen vast tracts of the United States. Among the locations in which he had served were San Diego Barracks in California, Fort Clark in Texas, and Fort Columbus in New York. As was the case with many of his countrymen, his military career had not always gone smoothly. A November 1859 return for Fort Columbus records that Gibbons, at that point a member of Company I, 1st US Artillery, was awaiting trial for desertion. The issue had been resolved by early the following year, when the Irishman was recorded as awaiting transfer to Company E of the 1st Artillery. The Galwegian made his fateful move to Fort Moultrie in South Carolina on 18 February 1860.[25]

It was around 7 a.m. on the morning of 12 April 1861 when Major Anderson finally decided the time had come for Fort Sumter to reply to the Confederate barrage. Captain Abner Doubleday of New York, who would rise to the rank of major-general of Volunteers during the coming war, was the man who would give the order to fire the first shot in defence of the Union. He later described the circumstances:

> As I was the ranking officer, I took the first detachment, and marched them to the casemates, which looked out upon the powerful iron-clad battery of Cummings Point. In aiming the first gun fired against the rebellion I had no

feeling of self-reproach, for I fully believed that the contest was inevitable, and was not of our seeking … My first shot bounded off from the sloping roof of the battery opposite without producing any apparent effect. It seemed useless to attempt to silence the guns there; for our metal was not heavy enough to batter the work down, and every ball glanced harmlessly off, except one, which appeared to enter an embrasure and twist the iron shutter, so as to stop the firing of that particular gun. I observed that a group of the enemy had ventured out from their intrenchments to watch the effect of the fire, but I sent them flying back to their shelter by the aid of a forty-two-pounder ball, which appeared to strike in among them.[26]

One of Doubleday's gun crew was none other than James Gibbons. He remembered:

The rebels opened on us just before daylight with a shot from Fort Johnson that came singing over our parapet. It was about two seconds before another came along, and then another, and another, until the 360 guns at Fort Johnson, Fort Moultrie, and Cumming's Point were playing upon us. It was about five o'clock when the Southerners began firing. It was seven o'clock, fully an hour after daylight, before we responded. We had only two companies there, E and H, of the First Regiment United States Artillery. The men and officers numbered seventy-one, and besides these there were sixteen laborers in the fort. Captain Doubleday had command of Company E, and was ordered by Major Anderson to fire on Cumming's Point. Captain Doubleday stood two feet behind me as I held the lanyard, and at his command I pulled it. It was a good shot, for it struck the wall at the Point, but the next shot, from the adjoining gun, was a better one. The rebels had laid a lot of railroad iron along the ramparts, and one of their men was walking on the slanting surface. The shot struck the iron, and the effect must have been prodigious, for the man who was walking over the iron shot up into the air and fell inside the walls of the fort. One of the bravest acts I ever saw happened about ten o'clock that morning. A shell from Fort Moultrie fell in the tower of our fort and rolled down the stairway to the ground. John Carroll, an old laborer from Baltimore, followed it down and was in the act of picking it up when his comrades called him to run away. Instead of running away, he coolly picked up the burning shell and threw it into a ditch, extinguishing the burning fuse. For this act of bravery he was handsomely complimented by the officers and applauded by his comrades.[27]

Although Gibbons claimed to be the man who pulled the lanyard to fire the first Union shot of the American Civil War, it remains unclear if this was actually the case. Regardless, he was certainly intimately involved in that momentous occasion. Despite their spirited response to the Confederate fire, the garrison in Fort Sumter was fighting a losing battle. At 2.30 p.m. the next day, 13 April 1861, Major Anderson agreed to surrender the fort to the Confederate commander Brigadier-General P.G.T. Beauregard. Incredibly, although around a thousand shots had been fired by Fort Sumter, which in turn had been the target of 3,341 projectiles, no soldiers were killed on either side during the blistering exchange. The terms of surrender agreed were generous towards the fort's defenders, and Major Anderson was given permission to depart with his garrison on the ships (including the *Pawnee* commanded by Stephen Rowan) that had initially come to resupply them. The date for the evacuation was set for the following day, Sunday 14 April.[28]

The early afternoon of 14 April arrived, and a small steamer, the *Isabel*, moved towards Fort Sumter in order to take the men and their belongings to the waiting Federal ships. As the garrison prepared to lower the stars and stripes over the fort for the final time, Major Anderson arranged for a 100-gun salute to be fired in honour of the flag. Cartridges had been sewn that morning in preparation for the event, which was to be overseen by Lieutenant Hall. The artillery pieces facing out towards the Atlantic were selected to perform the duty, and the cartridges were stacked beside the pieces in readiness. The salute started at around 2.30 p.m., and the nearby Confederates waited for the ceremony to end before moving out to take possession of their prize. As the firing reached the halfway mark, Private Daniel Hough, a former farmer from Co. Tipperary, was in the process of ramming a cartridge bag into the muzzle of his gun when suddenly the powder exploded prematurely. The blast ripped off the thirty-three-year-old's right arm, throwing him to the ground like a ragdoll.

Hough was another ten-year veteran, having first enlisted in 1849. During the course of his service the normally quiet soldier had begun to develop emotional problems. In 1857 while stationed in Florida his commanding officer felt that he was 'so crazy as to be unmanageable and I would respectfully recommend that he be sent to an Insane Asylum'. A medical examiner stated that Hough experienced episodes where he became 'violent and unruly, assaulting anyone that might be in his way'. He received treatment in St Elizabeth's Hospital for the Insane in Washington in the summer of 1857, but was returned to his unit, supposedly cured, that September. The emotionally troubled Irishman's difficulties ended with the explosion at Fort Sumter. His death had been almost instantaneous, making Daniel Hough the first soldier to be killed in the American Civil War. He was buried later that day on Fort Sumter's parade ground.[29]

The sparks from the blast that had killed Hough ignited the remaining cartridges beside the gun, blowing the five other members of its crew into the air. One of the men, Private George Pinchard, was a New Yorker; the four others were Irish. They were Waterford-born twenty-six-year-old Private George Fielding, twenty-two-year-old Private John Irwin from Limerick, thirty-year-old Private James Hays from Tyrone and twenty-year-old Private Edward Gallway of Cork. All five men were wounded, but the evacuation of the fort had to continue regardless. When the garrison marched out at 4.30 p.m., Pinchard, Irwin and Hays were carried to the waiting *Isabel* on mattresses. However, both Gallway and Fielding were too seriously injured to make the trip. They were taken to a hospital in Charleston, where George Fielding remained for six weeks before he was deemed well enough to return home. Edward Gallway did not join him. The Corkman died on the night of 14 April, and was buried in Charleston Cemetery, officially the second soldier to die in the American Civil War.[30]

The Irish had made such an impact on the pre-war US military that they were virtually omnipresent within it. They were there for some of the most important moments in American history, such as John Brown's raid and the firing on Fort Sumter. These Irishmen played a key role in the events that led to the American Civil War, but for some, such as Luke Quinn, Daniel Hough and Edward Gallway, their front row seats to history came at a terrible price.

Facing the first battle

After the firing on Fort Sumter both the North and South moved to mobilise resources and manpower for the coming struggle. In these early days many men enthusiastically enlisted, often more concerned about missing out on the action then being killed or maimed. Expectations that one battle would decide the war were commonplace, and both sides felt confident that they would sweep away their opponents. As the first major clash of the war loomed, Union and Confederate units began to converge on Washington DC and Virginia. They were often poorly equipped and many were clad in a dazzling array of uniform styles and colours.

On 21 July 1861 the day of reckoning finally came. Just over 60,000 men converged in northern Virginia to fight in what the Union called the Battle of Bull Run, but for the Confederates was the Battle of Manassas. Throughout the ranks on both sides were a large number of Irishmen. This is the story of three such men who fought for the Union; Private John Donovan, Captain James Haggerty and Corporal Owen McGough.

Of the three men only James Haggerty served in an ethnic Irish regiment. The 69th New York State Militia were the most famous Irish formation of their time, and among their ranks at Bull Run were leaders of the New York-Irish community such as Michael Corcoran (the 69th's Colonel) and Thomas Francis Meagher. Haggerty had been born in Glenswilly, Co. Donegal, around 1816, but had not taken the boat to the United States until well into his thirties, in 1849. A carpenter by trade, he set up his own business at 70 Bleeker Street in New York in 1856. He married Elisa Bentley from Limerick, and in 1858 the couple celebrated the birth of their first daughter, Anne. Tragedy struck when the girl died after only three days, but a year later a healthy second daughter, Rosina, was born. Despite living in the United States James was a dedicated Fenian and kept in touch with affairs in Ireland. He had originally joined the Militia to gain military experience in the hope of one day returning to participate in a rebellion in his native country. He had already served as a lieutenant-colonel in the 75th Regiment prior to its disbandment in 1856, and when Michael Corcoran was made Colonel of the 69th New York State Militia in 1859 he asked Haggerty to become captain of Company A. The Donegal man was a popular officer and a strict disciplinarian – his company became known as 'Haggerty's Bullies'. When the first shots were fired on Fort Sumter in April 1861 and President Abraham Lincoln called for volunteers, James Haggerty and the 69th New York State Militia had answered.[31]

Little is known about Private John Donovan's life prior to Bull Run, although the emigrant had chosen to move west to the challenging environment of Minnesota to make a home. It was in Houston, Minnesota that the Irishman enlisted on 22 May 1861, in what would become the 2nd Wisconsin Infantry. Fate would draw both Haggerty and Donovan's regiments into the same brigade; both the 69th New York State Militia and 2nd Wisconsin would fight the battle under the overall command of Colonel William Tecumseh Sherman. Unlike John Donovan, Owen McGough was not an 1861 volunteer. The Co. Monaghan native had been born around 1827, and had arrived in New York in 1845. His passage was most likely aboard the ship *Pacific* via Liverpool, where Owen was listed as one of nine members of the McGough family aboard. He had worked as a teamster before deciding on a life in the regular army as a means of gaining secure employment. On his enlistment in Cornwall, New York, in 1859 he was recorded as being 5ft 6½ins in height, with blue eyes, brown hair and a fair complexion. He went into action on 21 July not far from James Haggerty and John Donovan, as a member of Battery D, 5th US Artillery.[32]

The campaign began when Union Brigadier-General Irvin McDowell marched his army out from Washington on 16 July to bring the Confederate force under Brigadier-General P.G.T. Beauregard to battle. The Rebel Army was drawn up behind a small creek called Bull Run to the north-east of Manassas Junction; McDowell decided to try to cross the creek and attack the enemy's left flank. To this end on the morning of 21 July the main body of the Union Army moved upstream to Sudley Ford, where they crossed and engaged the Confederate left at Matthews Hill. While the fighting got underway Sherman's brigade, which contained both Haggerty's and Donovan's units, were left holding Stone Bridge across Bull Run creek. The day of battle found James Haggerty as acting lieutenant-colonel of the 69th, due to an injury which had incapacitated the regular post holder, Robert Nugent. The fighting initially went well for the Northern forces, and as the Confederates were pushed back from their position on Matthews Hill, Sherman was ordered across Bull Run creek to add his brigade's weight to the attack. James Haggerty and John Donovan were about to go into action for the first time.

Officers of the 69th New York State Militia just before the First Battle of Bull Run. Among the group are Michael Corcoran and Thomas Francis Meagher. James Haggerty is almost certainly one of these men, but has not yet been identified. (Library of Congress)

As the 69th New York State Militia, 2nd Wisconsin and the other men of Sherman's brigade (the 13th and 79th New York State Militia) splashed across the creek in the late morning of 21 July, their advance brought them up in the rear of some of the retreating Rebels who were trying to gain their new position atop Henry Hill. Immediately on crossing the stream and entering the meadow on the other side, they found that the woods in their front were full of the retreating enemy. William Tecumseh Sherman describes what happened next: 'Lieutenant-Colonel Haggerty, of the Sixty-ninth, without orders, rode out and endeavored to intercept their retreat. One of the enemy, in full view, at short range, shot Haggerty, and he fell dead from his horse.' Perhaps incensed at what had just happened, the 69th opened fire on the retreating Rebels, who replied in kind. Sherman ordered the firing ceased as he was determined to move his brigade up to join with the main attack. Captain James Kelly of the 69th related that Haggerty was 'killed by a Louisiana Zouave, whom he pursued as the latter was on his retreat with his regiment into the woods, and several of our men were severely wounded.' If Kelly is right in his assessment then it is possible that Haggerty fell at the hands of a fellow Irishman, as many of the Louisiana Zouaves were of Irish origin. James Haggerty's active military career had ended almost before it had begun, leaving a widowed wife and infant daughter behind in New York.[33]

Unlike Haggerty, John Donovan had escaped this first encounter with the enemy unscathed. However, his luck was about to run out. As Sherman's brigade advanced with the main Union force they were thrown into the struggle to overpower the Confederate positions on top of Henry Hill. Donovan describes his ordeal as he advanced:

> Marched up the hill after getting over a fence, and on reaching nearly to the brow I was struck by a rifle ball in the calf of my right leg, outside, passing through to the skin on the other side … I stepped back to the fence, sat down

and bound up my leg to keep it from bleeding. I then got up and loaded and fired from where I stood. After firing three times, another ball hit me in the left heel, glancing up along near my ankle joint … After being hit the second time I still kept loading and firing as fast as I could. In about ten minutes, as near as I can judge, a third ball struck me in the right side … This disabled me somewhat for a short time, but I again loaded and fired two or three times as well as I could, when I was struck in the right arm (while in the act of firing) about midway between my elbow and shoulder joints, the ball running up towards my neck … I fired my musket but once after this, as the recoil of it hurt my shoulder so, I was unable to bear it. I then left the fence to get behind a tree standing some two hundred and fifty yards off, and picked up a revolver which lay on the ground, just after I left the fence, at which time a bullet struck on my right wrist glancing off from the bone. I went a little further towards the tree, when some twelve or fifteen Confederate soldiers came out of the woods directly towards me. I fired the revolver at them three times, and just as I fired the third barrel, a bullet fired by one of this company struck me just below my left eye, going into my head.[34]

By this point Donovan had been struck an incredible six times, and was left for dead on the field. As Donovan was being repeatedly hit, his fellow Irishman, Owen McGough, was also experiencing a whirlwind of fire. His Battery D was commanded by Captain Charles Griffin, while the Monaghan mans artillery section was led by Lieutenant Adelbert Ames; both would go on to become generals before war's end. Lieutenant Ames was hit in the thigh at the outset of the battle, but refused to leave his post. Ames, McGough and the rest of the gun crew made their way forward with their gun as Captain Griffin redeployed a number of times, on each occasion moving closer and closer to the Confederate positions on Henry Hill. As the fire intensified, two more of the crew fell, one dead and one (Sergeant Murphy) wounded. The final position of the gun was almost on top of Henry Hill itself, and the artillerymen felt the full brunt of the Rebel fire. A round struck the gun, killing Patrick Sullivan, another of the crew, and destroying the wheel. Confederate infantry then began to charge towards the gun, which was without any support. As bullets whizzed by and with the enemy closing in, McGough desperately sought to save the gun by replacing the mangled wheel with a spare. He succeeded just in time, and along with Ames and the survivors succeeded in carrying the piece off the field. It was the only one of Captain Griffin's six guns to escape capture that day.[35]

As the battle had raged on into late afternoon, Confederate reinforcements had arrived and assailed the Union right flank, forcing it back and eventually precipitating a headlong retreat. The Rebels had won the day, though the fight had not been the glorious affair that many on both sides had expected. The Battle of Bull Run was but a taste of what was to come in the years ahead.

As the Confederates celebrated their victory, at least one man on the field was still unaware of the result. John Donovan remained where he had fallen; knocked senseless by the final wound he had received. It was midday the day after the battle before he regained consciousness:

> When I came to I found myself lying right where I fell the day before. I tried to get up, but could not. After this I made several ineffectual attempts to crawl away to the shade of a tree, the sun shining very hot. About four p.m., a couple of soldiers came along, picked me up, and carried me to the cars, and I was sent to Richmond, afterwards sent to Alabama, and finally released on parole.

John Donovan had survived, but his fighting days were over. He would never recover from the debilitating effects of his injuries. Writing afterwards he described the consequences of the six bullets that had struck him:

> The bullet still remains in my head; the hospital surgeon says it lies somewhere near my right ear (the sense of hearing being entirely lost in that ear), the drum, or tympanum having being injured by it. The slightest touch on my chin, or near it, causes a severe pain in my right temple and over the ear. I cannot see at all with my left eye. I cannot bear to be out in the sun; it makes me dizzy and my head pains me severely; so also does more than ordinary exercise. Ordinarily, when sitting quiet, my head only occasionally troubles me – a little dizziness and heaviness is about all – except when out in the sun or heated, as before stated; and also when I attempt to lift anything, it puts me in severe pain in my head, and my eyes pain me exceedingly, as well then as when heated or out in the sun. I am obliged to keep out of the sun as much as possible on account of this excruciating pain in my head and eyes, and when I read my eyes fill with water, and I have to rest. I cannot write a letter of ordinary length. I have to stop several times for this and from dizziness. There is occasionally a dimness comes over my right eye even when quiet, but not very often.[36]

It is apparent from the way Donovan described his injuries that they were having a colossal impact on his life. The same was true for Elisa Haggerty and her daughter Rosina who had lost a husband and father in the fight. James Haggerty had been the first member of the 69th New York State Militia to be killed at Bull Run. In place of the family breadwinner they received a pension for James's service which would continue to pay out until 1914, over fifty years after his death. Aside from this all that was left to the family were the eulogies of Haggerty's comrades in arms, among whom was Thomas Francis

The ruins of the Henry House on Henry Hill, part of the First Bull Run battlefield. This hill was held by the Confederates and was the target of the Irishmen's units during the engagement. (Library of Congress)

Meagher. Later that year the orator who had commanded Company K of the 69th at Bull Run made the following comments about the Donegal man:

> … Prominent amongst them, strikingly noticeable by reason of his large, iron frame, and the boldly chiselled features, on which the impress of great strength of will and intellect was softened by a constant play of humor and the goodness and grand simplicity of his heart-wrapped in his rough overcoat, with his sword crossed upon his breast, his brow boldly uplifted as though he were still in command, and the consciousness of having done his duty sternly to the last still animating the Roman face – there lies James Haggerty – a braver soldier than whom the land of Sarsfield and Shields has not produced, and whose name, worked in gold upon the colors of the Sixty-ninth, should be henceforth guarded with all the jealousy and pride which inspires a regiment, wherever its honor is at stake and its standards are in peril.[37]

The Battle of Bull Run would live long in the memory of Owen McGough as well. Although he had not been wounded in the fight, his brush with death must have had a profound impact on him. He survived his wartime service and was awarded the Congressional Medal of Honor for his actions during the battle. On 28 August 1897, just over thirty-eight years after the actions which inspired it, he was presented with the award which was accompanied with the following citation: 'Through his personal exertions under a heavy fire, one of the guns of his battery was brought off the field; all the other guns were lost.'[38]

Despite the length of time that elapsed before he was presented with the medal, McGough's represents the earliest action in the war for which an Irishman was awarded the Medal of Honor.

The Battle of Bull Run on 21 July 1861 would be dwarfed by the scale and carnage of later engagements. Nonetheless, it did represent the first indication that the war may be prolonged and bloody, and for some, including many Irishmen, their war started and ended on that Sunday in July. For thousands of individuals such as John Donovan and Owen McGough and families like Elisa and Rosina Haggerty, this first major battle of the American Civil War would never be eclipsed, and its effects would stay with them for decades.

Recruiting for the Irish Brigade

There were many different factors that motivated Irishmen to enlist during the American Civil War – for some it was patriotism or a thirst for adventure, others sought military experience in the hope of one day liberating Ireland, and for more it was simply a matter of economics. These reasons changed as the war progressed, as the harsh realities of life and death on the battlefield became clear to all. However, the carnage of later years was still in the future in 1861, when Irishmen chose to join up in their thousands. What persuaded them to do so?

At first glance it would seem that many of those who emigrated to the northern United States had little reason to find common cause with the Union, particularly in cities where the Irish had endured hostility and racism in the years before 1861. The main thorn in their side had been a political movement known as the American Party, better remembered today by their nickname, the 'Know-Nothings'. The Know-Nothings were virulently anti-Catholic and anti-immigrant, and in the ever increasing Irish population they found one of their main targets. When the new Republican Party was formed in 1854, many former Know-Nothings decided to join its ranks, and it was as a Republican that Abraham Lincoln was elected to the Presidency in 1860. As Irish

Catholics tended to support the pro-immigrant Democratic Party, it might be expected that there would be little initial enthusiasm for Lincoln's 1861 call for volunteers to suppress the rebellion. Despite this, significant numbers of Irishmen did enlist to fight for the Union in the early part of the war. The newspapers of the time offer us a window into what was being said to Irishmen in 1861 to inspire and motivate them in the cause of Union.[39]

The autumn of 1861 in New York was the scene of a major recruitment drive, as efforts stepped up to fill the first three regiments of what would become known as the Irish Brigade. The genesis of the project had come from within the Irish community itself, who wanted the brigade to represent them on the battlefield. It eventually travelled to the front as the 63rd, 69th and 88th New York Volunteer Infantry, and would later add regiments from the Irish communities of Massachusetts and Pennsylvania. Together they would go on to become one of the most famous brigades to serve in the American Civil War. In 1861 the ranks still needed to be filled, and advertisements like this one ran in local newspapers, informing men where they could join up:

> 69th, OR FIRST REGIMENT IRISH BRIGADE. Co. I of this Regt. is recruiting at 44 Prince Street. A few more young men wanted to complete the Company. Uniforms, Rations, and Quarters furnished on signing the roll.[40]

These were the days before mass media, and it was through newspapers and public meetings that recruiters sought to encourage their fellow Irishmen into the military fold. On 5 October the *Irish-American*'s readers were notified of a major event, planned to assist with manning the Irish Brigade:

THE IRISH BRIGADE
FOR THE AMERICAN UNION!

IN AID OF THIS PATRIOTIC ORGANIZATION, THOMAS FRANCIS MEAGHER will deliver an Oration in the Academy of Music, cor. 14th street and Irving-place, Sunday evening, October 6th, on the IRISH SOLDIER his history and present Duty – his Obligations to the American Republic:- The National Cause, its justice, sanctity and grandeur. The memories of the National Flag, and its promised glory. The triumph of the National Arms assured! The New World vindicates itself against the Old!

A Splendid Military Band will be in attendance. Doors open at half past six o'clock, p.m. Oration to commence at eight o'clock precisely. Tickets of Admission 25 cents, Reserved Seats 50 cents. To be had at the Academy of Music; Hall & Sons, Broadway; Kirker's 599 Broadway; Haverty's 112 Fulton-street; and at the IRISH-AMERICAN Office, 32 Beekman Street.[41]

The purpose of the event was twofold: raise funds for the brigade and prompt additional recruits to come forward. If the military band was not enough to draw the crowds, the presence of Thomas Francis Meagher on the bill assured the event's success. Meagher was not only the driving force behind the move to organise the brigade, he was also Ireland's most famous orator. The Waterford native had achieved fame in his homeland through his involvement with the Young Ireland movement and the failed 1848 rising, which had seen him deported to Van Diemen's Land (now Tasmania). Having escaped captivity in 1852 he went to the United States, where he became one of the leaders of the Irish community in New York. During his time in Ireland he had earned the sobriquet 'Meagher of the Sword', not as a result of military prowess, but because of his stirring 'Sword Speech' of 1846, in which he

A typical recruiting station in New York in 1861. (Library of Congress)

expressed the view that violent struggle was a legitimate way to secure repeal of the Act of Union. Now Meagher was turning his considerable talents to encouraging his countrymen to enlist in the cause of Union.

The venue for Meagher's speech – the Academy of Music – had opened in 1854 and was by all accounts an impressive setting. It had been fitted with 2,200 iron chairs with spring seats, designed to fold up when not in use – the very latest in comfort and design. The stage from which he would speak was 30ft high and 35ft wide, and the entire Academy could seat 4,000 people. The balmy evening of Sunday 6 October arrived, and at the designated time the theatre was overflowing with the city's Irish community. Those lucky enough to be in attendance were greeted by a stage bedecked with both the flag of the United States and the green banner of Ireland. The military band kicked the evening off, playing well-known Irish and American tunes to excite the crowd. At 8 p.m. a prominent Irish-American, Judge Charles Daly, came forward to introduce the main attraction. Dressed in black broadcloth, Thomas Francis Meagher emerged to a thunderous ovation that continued for several minutes. The master speaker prepared to address his audience.[42]

Somewhat surprisingly for an orator of such renown, Meagher read his speeches rather than delivering them from memory. This was just as well on this occasion, as he intended to continue for no less than two hours. It is hard today to picture Meagher's speaking style, which must have been extremely impressive to keep thousands of people enraptured for such a period of time. One witness described him as speaking with 'little energy', preferring to concentrate on getting his sentences right. He reserved gesturing to key moments in his speech, and when he did use his hands he favoured quick and decisive movements in order to emphasise his point. Perhaps Meagher's greatest asset was his quick wit, which he took every opportunity to employ throughout the evening.[43]

The advantage for Meagher in preparing a lecture in advance was that he could carefully craft its content to have the maximum impact on his audience. At the Academy of Music his aim was to excite the martial spirit of the attendees and to support the Irish Brigade, both financially and through enlistment. By examining the content of what Meagher spoke about that October night we can gain some insight into what motivated Irishmen in 1861 New York. So what did he say?

Meagher dedicated the first part of his presentation to the military achievements of the Irish soldier through history. He quickly elicited cheers from the thronged hall by reminding the crowd of the 'Shamrocks and the Lillies … blended on the banners of France', as he noted the exploits of Wild Geese regiments such as Burke's, Dillon's and Clare's. Next he cited the Irish in Spanish service, and those who had assisted in the liberation of Chile, Bolivia and Venezuela. Despite his political views on England and the English, Meagher had no hesitation in recording the heavy Irish involvement in British armies from the 'burning jungles of Hindostan' to the 'harsh sterilities of the Crimea'. He even made special mention of the performance of the Connaught Rangers in Spain during the Peninsular War. The purpose of Meagher's historical military tour quickly became apparent as he drove home his point:

> Enough for me to say – enough for any one to say – that, whilst in other lands, in other generations, under other circumstances, whether they be considered humiliating or exalting, the Irish soldier has fought manfully and brilliantly – here, at last – here, on this Continent – here, at these very doors – here, at this very hour, he has presented to him, and invoking the services of his trenchant sword, a cause, the justice, the righteousness, the sanctity, the grandeur of which can neither be exaggerated nor impeached.

This passage raised the roof of the Academy. Meagher had already highlighted that the Irish were now American citizens, and here he explained that they had been presented with an opportunity to repeat the feats of previous generations in a righteous cause. His next aim was to explain to the assembled masses exactly what that cause was. Meagher described the Union as a country which provided a guarantee of an order of society and government which was the envy of the world – a republic where anyone had an opportunity to advance, no matter what their background. Here Meagher sought to remind his audience that even though they had suffered continued discrimination during the preceding decade, it was nothing in comparison to the conditions they had endured at home in Europe. In the Union they had a voice – they could vote, they could practice their religion and customs – they could seek to better themselves and their community. Meagher summed up the threat the Confederacy posed to this way of life:

… you all know – the world knows – that the authority of this Executive [the Union Government] has been violently questioned … it has been insolently and murderously assailed. Who proceeds against it with fire and sword, and, striking at it with all the art of the assassin, and all the ferocity of the bruiser, strikes radically and vitally against the people from whose free will and spontaneous votes that Executive has sprung.

As Meagher continued he was at pains to point out to his audience that the South had been threatening aggression for a long time, and had failed to give Abraham Lincoln any chance to prove himself in office. Given the general Irish dislike for the Republican Party, it is interesting to note Meagher's comments in relation to Lincoln:

… Abraham Lincoln took the [Presidential] oath administered to him … and thereby bound himself with a sacred emphasis to support the laws and the Constitution of the United States … I firmly believe that at that very moment the platform upon which he had been presented for election, sunk and vanished from his view …

In other words whatever Lincoln had said prior to becoming President and whatever his personal views with regards to issues such as slavery, these were no longer relevant, as he would uphold the Constitution and laws on behalf of everyone in the nation. Although Meagher framed this statement in terms of unreasonable Southerners unwilling to give Lincoln a chance, he was just as eager to convince his overwhelmingly Democratic Irish audience. Meagher went further still, attacking some of those Northerners whom he viewed as exacerbating the problems with the South, particularly abolitionists and former Know-Nothings. He was well aware that elements in the Irish community felt this was

Thomas Francis Meagher in the uniform of a Brigadier-General of Volunteers, when he was commanding the Irish Brigade. (Library of Congress)

not their war, and that some Irish-Democrats were encouraging men not to enlist as a result. It was also apparent that at this stage of the war there was significant sympathy in Ireland for the Confederate position. Meagher dealt with these arguments by reminding his listeners that whatever the causes of unrest between North and South, the violent actions of the seceded states were utterly unjustified. He also made clear that anyone in Ireland who was commenting on the situation was at too far a remove to have any real knowledge of events in America, and had no entitlement to cast judgement. He reiterated that the preservation and protection of the Union was of the utmost importance to the future of the Irish both in the United States and in Ireland:

> … if this great Republic, frank and liberal to an excess as it is in all its requirements and provisions, is not to be upheld – upheld with the stoutest arm and the fullest heart – then, I say, there is no hope for manhood and humanity elsewhere – least of all, is there hope for Ireland, which has had from this Republic, in the direst extremities of the Irish race, the promptest, the staunchest, and the most plenteous succor.

He recognised the need to win over those Irish still undecided about the conflict, and time and again took the opportunity to reinforce the value of the Union in what was a central theme in his oration. He asked the assembled crowds:

> … Is it necessary for me to remind my countrymen that … here, and here alone, can the Irish race – ceasing to be a race of emigrants and exiles and becoming citizens, reconstruct itself as a political power, and so retrieve in some measure its historic reputation.

Meagher continued to attack those in the South – often in a fashion that elicited great laughter from the audience – and drew on another image of Southerners that did not appeal to the Irish of the Northern states. Describing those in power in the South as an 'aristocracy of nigger-nourished planters' he was presenting a view that the Southern states were creating a social order akin to that seen in the aristocracies of Europe, where a landed gentry class exerted authority over the rest of the population. In Meagher's view this was far removed from the more egalitarian situation in the Northern states, and it would also have seemed worryingly similar to the social structure then in force in Ireland. The South's position as a major cotton producer also had a bearing, as Britain needed vast amounts of cotton to run her cotton mills. At the commencement of the war this manifested itself in significant pro-Confederate feeling in Britain, and this fact was seized on by Meagher as a recruiting tool. Irish recruiters could argue that a weakened Union would be unable to stem British power and would therefore lessen the likelihood that the United States could be a source of aid to Ireland in the future. On a more basic level, though, Meagher was also seeking to tie the cause of the Confederacy to Britain, as can be seen with another question he posed to the crowd:

> … Is it necessary for me to remind my countrymen that England is with the South, and that every blow dealt against the insurrectionists is a blow dealt against the oppressor, plunderer and calumniator of the Irish race?

The war was an opportunity for the Irish community to show their commitment to their new nation, and to make it clear to their detractors that despite how they may be viewed they were going to fully uphold the constitution of their adopted country. Meagher made it very clear why he had come to speak to his countrymen in the Academy of Music:

… I am here tonight, within these splendid walls, to evoke a declaration from the Democracy of the first city in the New World which shall silence these [the South's] denunciations, and assure the Government at Washington that, at all events, they shall have the Irish arm and the Irish heart – the Irish heart with all its warmth, and the Irish arm with all its nerve – until the National Sovereignty conquers and prevails.

The wild applause this statement received from those inside the Academy made it clear that the gifted orator had succeeded in wooing what was undoubtedly a receptive audience. As the event drew to a close, the famous revolutionary leader wanted to explain to his fellow Irish why he was not advocating the radical course chosen by the South. Simply put, he did not believe such a course was necessary in the United States:

A revolutionist in Ireland, I am a conservative in America … And Why? Because here the progress and dreams of the revolutionist have been realised, and he finds those avenues to fortune, renown, social happiness and political power thrown wide open to him which in the old world were beset with so many impediments or were inexorably closed …

At the conclusion of the event 'long and continued' cheers rang out as Meagher withdrew from the stage. As the thousands of attendees dispersed, journalists from the majority of the city's major newspapers dashed off to file reports on the speech, and its noticeable effect on the crowd. For those unable to read or write, Meagher's key points would have been relayed by word of mouth in the streets and taverns frequented by the Irish community.[44]

It is impossible to measure the effectiveness of an event such as the Academy of Music oration for recruitment into the Irish Brigade, though it seems likely given the all-pervasive war fever in these early months that it met with some success. Undoubtedly a number of young men who crowded into the venue that night were persuaded by the brilliance of Meagher's oratory, and went off to become Irish-American soldiers for the Union. Thomas Francis Meagher would go on to command the Irish Brigade in the field, but the enthusiasm he witnessed among the Academy of Music crowd would become a distant memory in the coming struggle. By late 1862, amid rising casualties in units such as the Irish Brigade and announcements such as the Emancipation Proclamation, the Irish community became increasingly disenfranchised by the war effort. Despite his efforts to do so, Meagher would never again be able to rekindle the passion he elicited in 1861 from the Irish of New York.

Following them home

The 'green flag' regiments of the Union Army remain the most recognisable expression of Irish involvement in the American Civil War. These ethnic units were proud of their heritage and sought to combine this with their loyalty to the Union, often by carrying green banners together with the national flag, or by bearing epithets such as the 'Irish Brigade'. But how 'Irish' were these regiments? How many men were Irish emigrants, and where in Ireland were they from? How many were Irish-American and how many had no connection to Ireland? One way of examining this is to look at where the men of a regiment were born.

One of these Union Irish regiments was the 23rd Illinois Infantry, 'Mulligan's Irish Brigade'. When the Civil War began in 1861 Irish-American James Adelbert Mulligan decided to form an Irish unit.

Mulligan had been born on 25 June 1830 in Utica, New York and had later moved to Chicago. He was educated at the University of St Mary's of the Lake in that city, and spent time as a lawyer and newspaper editor before the war. As an active member of the Democratic Party, he was an influential member of Illinois's Irish community. In order to draw recruits in 1861, he had the following announcement placed in the *Chicago Tribune*:

> Rally! All Irishmen in favour of forming a Regiment of Irish Volunteers to sustain the Government of the United States in and through the present war, will rally at North Market Hall, this evening [April 20] at 7½ o'clock. Come all. For the honor of the Old Land, rally. Rally for the defense of the new.[45]

The regiment that Mulligan raised became the 23rd Illinois Infantry, and the Irish-American was installed as its Colonel. It was made up of a total of ten companies. Seven were from Cook County, Illinois and represented men from Chicago's Irish community; LaSalle County and Grundy County provided a company each, with the final company being organised in Detroit, Michigan. A number of the companies had been raised from pre-war Irish militia units, most notably the Shields Guards from Chicago, who made up Companies I and K. They were named for Tyrone native and prominent Illinois Democrat James Shields, and had been formed in 1854. The Shields Guards were the first military company from Chicago to offer their services to the Federal Government.[46]

After training, the 23rd had their first taste of the war in Missouri. In September 1861 they were besieged in the town of Lexington by a Confederate Army under Sterling Price. Outnumbered and surrounded by the Rebel force, the Union troops were forced to surrender after some stiff fighting – the 23rd Illinois had been captured in their first

James Adelbert Mulligan, who raised the 23rd Illinois Infantry and was killed in action at the Second Battle of Kernstown, Virginia in 1864. (Library of Congress)

battle. The men of the regiment were paroled and had to await exchange for a like number of Confederate captives before they could return to active duty. Colonel Mulligan was himself exchanged on 30 October 1861. Difficulties with organising the exchange led to the original 23rd being disbanded, although Mulligan succeeded in having it restored to service in December. He immediately set about re-raising the regiment with additional recruits and men from the original unit so it could enter the fray once more.[47]

Early in 1862 the 23rd served as guards to Rebel prisoners at Camp Douglas near Chicago. They moved to the Eastern Theater of war in June 1862, where they spent the majority of the conflict in western Virginia engaged in quelling guerrilla activities. Their war arrived in earnest when they formed part of the Union forces engaged in the Shenandoah Valley Campaign of 1864, where Colonel Mulligan was killed at the Second Battle of Kernstown on 24 July. The regiment was consolidated into five companies in August of that year, and went on to serve in the Petersburg and Appomattox Campaigns before being mustered out in Chicago in July 1865. During the war the regiment lost four officers and fifty men killed or mortally wounded, and a further two officers and ninety-three men died of disease.[48]

A number of the regiment received the Medal of Honor for gallantry during the conflict. Private John Creed of Company D, a carpenter born in Ireland, captured a Confederate flag at the Battle of Fisher's Hill on 22 September 1864. He received his award on 6 October the same year. Corporal Patrick Highland (Hyland), also of Company D, was a professional soldier from County Tipperary. On 2 April 1865 he showed conspicuous gallantry during the assault on Fort Gregg on the Petersburg Front, as he acted as color-bearer during the action. His medal was issued on 2 April 1865.[49]

The 23rd Illinois had undergone multiple reorganisations during the war. It was at its most 'Irish' in 1861, before it's engagement and capture at Lexington. As the war progressed and the demand for manpower

The charge of the 23rd Illinois at the Battle of Lexington in 1861, as depicted by *Harper's Weekly*. (*Harper's Weekly*)

intensified, many ethnic regiments, including the 23rd, received recruits with no particular ethnic attachment to the unit. This was particularly prevalent in 1864 and 1865 as casualty rates soared.[50]

Of course, the place where a soldier was born does not provide definitive evidence for his ethnicity. A New York or Canadian-born Irishman would in many cases have had just as strong a sense of his 'Irishness' as someone born in Ireland. The Colonel of the 23rd Illinois, James Mulligan, is a case in point. This was particularly true of the years prior to the Civil War when anti-Irish sentiment had a binding effect on members of the Irish-American community.

There are 1,585 men listed as having served with the 23rd Illinois Infantry in the American Civil War. The level of detail about where these men were born varies greatly, and is dependent on how accurate the enlisting officer chose to be. In the 23rd we know Private Thomas Ennes was a former newsboy from Newbridge, County Kildare – Private John

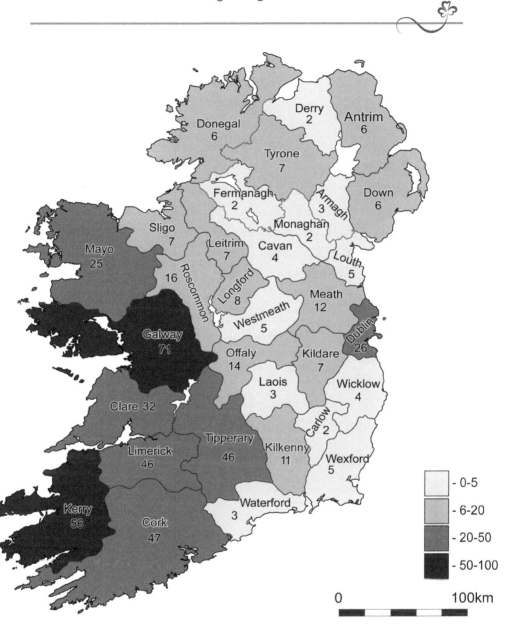

The breakdown of the counties in Ireland that contributed men to the 23rd Illinois Infantry, 'Mulligan's Irish Brigade'. (Illustrated by Sara Nylund)

Armstrong a merchant from Cootehill in County Monaghan – Private Patrick Shivers a laborer from Castledawson in County Derry and First Sergeant Thomas Killey a farmer from Craughwell in County Galway. However, the level of detail available on these men is the exception – for some soldiers no place of birth is recorded, and for others only their country is listed.[51]

Examining where the soldiers in the 23rd Illinois were from immediately reveals its strong Irish character. Over 50 per cent of the men for whom nationality information survives were born in Ireland. Of those remaining, the surnames of many suggest that although born in the United States they were most probably members of the Irish-American community. There are a number of cases where an older brother, born in Ireland, served with a younger brother who had been born in the United States. There were significantly more men in the regiment who had been born in Ireland (682) than in the United States (407). Of the American-born men, the majority had been born in New York rather than Illinois, and had travelled to that state either before the war or with the intent of enlisting there.[52]

Each of the ten companies in the regiment had a strong Irish-born contingent, but it was particularly noticeable in Company B, the Montgomery Guards (107), and Company F, the La Salle Guards (126). It is extremely fortunate that of the Irish-born, details on the county of origin survive for 496 of them. This shows that the 23rd Illinois Infantry had representatives from all across Ireland – there were men from each of the thirty-two counties serving in its ranks.[53]

While every county is represented, there is a noticeable concentration of men from the west and south-west of Ireland. Although these were some of the regions that suffered badly during the Famine of the 1840s, that alone does not explain the distribution pattern in the 23rd. Galway has the largest representation with seventy-one men, followed by Kerry with at least fifty-six of the regiment hailing from that county. It is interesting to consider if there were any community aspects at play among those who fought with the 23rd; emigrants from the same locality in Ireland often found themselves sharing the same community in the United States, and it seems probable that small groups of men from the same county may have then joined up to fight together. There is evidence for some concentrations like this in the 23rd Illinois. For example thirty-seven men from Kerry served in Company F, the La Salle Guards, while twenty-three men from Tipperary were in Company B, the Montgomery Guards.[54]

Among the more unusual places of birth were two soldiers who had been born at sea while their parents made the trip to the United States. There were also those in the 23rd Illinois who had no connection with Ireland and the Irish-American community. Much of Europe had some representation – there were small numbers of men from England, Germany, Scotland, France, Norway, Sweden, Switzerland, Wales and the Netherlands in Mulligan's Irish Brigade. These men had no obvious reason to seek out an Irish regiment to join, and it is probable that they enrolled in one of its companies as they lived nearby or were drafted into the unit later in the war.[55]

The proportion of Irish-born men who served in 23rd Illinois during the war would certainly have been higher had the regiment not been temporarily disbanded in 1861 and subsequently reorganised. Analysis undertaken by James B. Swan on another Irish regiment, the 90th Illinois Infantry or 'Chicago's Irish Legion', bears this out. In that unit of the 950 non-commissioned officers and men who served, almost 70 per cent were of Irish birth. It is probable that other Irish regiments such as those in New York and Massachusetts had similar if not higher percentages of Irish-born soldiers in the ranks.[56]

The strong Irish-born presence in the 23rd Illinois was one of the elements that gave the unit its Irish character. However, these men were not only Irish but often from the same regions of Ireland; as a result large numbers of men from places like Galway, Kerry, Limerick, Tipperary and Cork served together in Mulligan's unit. In many instances they must have not only shared a country of birth, but a common memory of the area in Ireland from which they came. Undoubtedly many a campfire in Missouri and Virginia between 1861 and 1865 witnessed shared reminiscences about hearth and home in the far away farms, villages and towns of west and south-west Ireland.

Realities

As the Civil War moved into 1862 it became clear that it was going to extract a frightening cost in human life. The first great battle of the conflict to demonstrate this was fought at Shiloh, Tennessee, in April that year. But worse was to come. At Antietam, Maryland, on 17 September the carnage was so great that it still represents the bloodiest day in American history. Hundreds of Irish were killed or wounded on both sides during the fighting, as soldiers fought back and forth across ground that would soon become imprinted on American memory, bearing names such as the 'Cornfield' and 'Bloody Lane.' The Eastern Theater witnessed another great battle around the town of Fredericksburg, Virginia, that December. In what was a disastrous defeat for Union arms, wave after wave of Yankees broke against the virtually impregnable Rebel positions on Marye's Heights. It was the scene where units such as the Irish Brigade won fame, but other Irishmen also excelled themselves in the fighting, and in doing so often paid a terrible price.

The war entered a new phase in 1864 when Ulysses S. Grant took command of all Union armies. For the first time coordinated offensives were launched in the Eastern and Western Theaters, as the North sought to take advantage of its superior logistics and manpower to bring the Confederacy to its knees. There would be no more retreat, and the months would pass in a whirlwind of almost constant combat. Casualty rates soared as the desperate struggle reached a crescendo. The ability to wage war on an industrial scale had been well honed by both sides, and now entire regiments could be decimated in a matter of moments. The war produced a number of Irish officers who demonstrated exceptional abilities to become leaders of men. Two of the best were from County Cork, one who fought with the Rebels and the other for the Yankees. Both won the admiration of their fellow officers and men, but neither would live to see the war's conclusion. Death in battle was not the only danger that faced Irish soldiers of the Civil War. Becoming a prisoner held its own dangers, and thousands died in camps far from the front lines. One Donegal man found himself having to endure captivity not once, but twice, as he struggled to survive some of the most barbaric conditions that the conflict imposed.

A Yankee and Rebel at Antietam

The Battle of Antietam on 17 September 1862 was the bloodiest day in United States history. From early morning until last light the Union Army of the Potomac and Confederate Army of Northern Virginia grappled with each other in a deadly contest around the farms and laneways surrounding Antietam Creek, on the outskirts of Sharpsburg, Maryland. By days end over 22,000 men had become casualties; more than 3,500 of them paid the ultimate price. The battle was the climax of Robert E. Lee's Maryland Campaign, the result of the first Confederate invasion of

Northern soil by the South which they hoped would bring the war to a conclusion. Among the regiments put through the meat-grinder that day was the Union Irish Brigade, which received devastating casualties during their attack on the position known as the 'Sunken Road.' However, the brigade was far from the only Irish representation on the field. Scattered across dozens of different outfits, both Yankee and Rebel, thousands of Irish soldiers fought and many died throughout that terrible day. Two of these men had the honour of leading their units onto the field on 17 September, and although fighting on opposite sides, both were destined to experience the maelstrom that was Antietam where the carnage was at its worst – The Miller Farm and Cornfield. For Colonel Howard Carroll of the 105th New York Infantry and Colonel Henry Strong of the 6th Louisiana Infantry, Antietam would prove to be their last battle.[57]

Dubliner Howard Carroll was born into a well to do family around the year 1827. As befitted a man whose mother was a relative of the Earl of Effingham, Howard received a fine education, studying at Trinity College, Dublin, from where he graduated in 1846. It was not until he was in his late twenties that he decided to try his hand on the other side of the Atlantic, when he emigrated to New York around 1855. As with many other Irishmen of all social classes, he found his way into the railroad business, spending the pre-war years working as a Civil Engineer for the New York Central Railroad. In contrast to Carroll, little is known about the circumstances by which Henry Strong found himself living in Louisiana. Indeed even the county of his birth remains obscure. He was born around 1827 and when war erupted in 1861, Henry was married and living in New Orleans, where he owned a coffeehouse and worked as a clerk. Both men were living in locations with a strong Irish presence; in 1860 New York State contained more Irish than anywhere else in the United States, with over 200,000 Irish in New York City alone, accounting for 26 per cent of the city's population – in the same year Louisiana was home to over 28,000 Irish, more than any other state in the South.[58]

Although Howard Carroll was not in an ethnic Irish regiment, like the majority of New York outfits the 105th had a strong Irish contingent, particularly in companies G, H and I recruited around Rochester. They had left for service in Virginia on 4 April 1862, and by the time of Antietam were veterans of battles at Cedar Mountain and Second Bull Run. The Dubliner had taken charge of the regiment in August, shortly after Cedar Mountain, when his predecessor, Colonel James Fuller, resigned.

Henry Strong had recruited the Calhoun Guards in New Orleans in 1861, and commanded them when they became part of the 6th Louisiana Infantry. The majority of the regiment was made up of Irishmen, and they had already served with Stonewall Jackson in the Shenandoah Valley and fought during the Seven Day's Battles and at Second Bull Run prior to the Maryland Campaign. As with his fellow countryman in Union blue, Henry Strong had risen to command of the 6th just prior to bloody clash outside Sharpsburg, in August 1862.[59]

At Antietam on the morning of 17 September Carroll and the 105th New York Infantry formed up with their brigade, under the command of Brigadier-General Abram Duryea, part of Joseph Hooker's Union First Corps. Hooker's men formed the right wing of the Army of the Potomac, and their task that morning was to commence the battle by assaulting the Confederate left. Howard Carroll's New Yorkers were placed on the left side of this attacking force, with orders to attack at first light. At around 6 a.m. the Dubliner ordered his troops forward, as the First Corps troops tramped slowly towards the enemy. They were pushing past a patch of woodland, today called the North Woods, when they came under Rebel artillery fire and sustained their first casualties. From here they advanced towards the edge of the Miller Cornfield, where the soldiers fanned out in line of battle, steeling themselves for the final advance. Although they were not to know it at the time, theirs was a position which by morning's end would be carpeted with the dead and dying. Colonel Carroll had remained mounted throughout so that his men could see him clearly, and to set an example for them. Now he and his men pushed southwards through the corn and into the Miller's open field beyond. It was here that they finally came face to face with the Rebels. A Georgian brigade under the command of Colonel Marcellus Douglass waited until the New Yorkers and their comrades emerged from the corn, before rising to their feet and unleashing a hail of lead into the faces of the Yankees, at a distance of only 250 yards. The 105th New York and the remainder of their brigade came to a shuddering halt in the face of this devastating fire. Regaining their composure, the 105th returned fire, and both sides stood and blazed away at each other, trading volleys of death. Eventually the murderous fire forced both lines to the ground in a desperate attempt to seek cover. As the minutes ticked agonisingly by it became clear that Duryea's brigade was not going to receive the support it needed; with Rebels now threatening to outflank them they had no option but to retreat back through the Miller Cornfield. The fighting had raged for some thirty minutes – in that time nearly a third of Duryea's force had become casualties. It had certainly been no place for a mounted officer. As his New Yorkers scampered back through the corn, Howard Carroll was already being carried wounded from the field – a minié ball in the left calf had brought his battle to a close.[60]

While Marcellus Douglass had been turning back Carroll and the other comrades in his brigade, Henry Strong and the 6th Louisiana were being moved to support the Georgians. They were part of the famed Louisiana Brigade of the Army of Northern Virginia, commanded at Antietam by Brigadier-General Harry T. Hays. The Louisianans had marched out of a patch of woods to the south-west of the Miller Cornfield (today the West Woods), across the Hagerstown Pike and into a ploughed field 300 yards behind Douglass and his men. The Irishmen lay down to reduce their exposure to Union artillery fire, but some of the shells still hit their mark. As the Union assault intensified, Douglass's Georgians became in desperate need of help. The 500 men of the Louisiana Brigade, including the 6th Louisiana, pressed forward to their assistance. They entered the fight and swept through and past the positions held by the Georgians, firing as they went, surging across the open field to the south of the Cornfield – Henry Strong was now fighting on the same ground that Howard Carroll had fallen on only moments earlier. By now Union troops were not only in the Cornfield to the north of the Confederates, they had also taken up a position in some woodland to the east (East Woods). While Colonel Strong and his men fought to push the Yankees back, they found themselves exposed to a deadly fire from both front and flank. As bullets and artillery fire rained in from the north and east, the Brigade advance stalled. Caught in such a horrendously exposed position, the 6th Louisiana and the rest of the brigade had no option but to withdraw. In a matter of minutes the Louisianans had been mangled. Of the 550 men Harry T. Hays had taken into the fight, 323 were casualties. The time was just after 7 a.m.; the Battle of Antietam was little more than an hour old.[61]

Henry Strong had taken the same view as his compatriot Howard Carroll when it came to advancing against the enemy – he chose to do so mounted. He had ridden forward with his men on a magnificent white horse, and in so doing became an almost instant target. Just after the 6th Louisiana entered the fighting, both Strong and his horse went down in a hail of bullets, in the south-east corner of the Miller's open field, south of the Cornfield and near the East Woods. Lieutenant George Ring of the regiment rushed to the Colonel's side, but by then it was already too late. Ring himself quickly became a casualty:

> I was struck with a ball on the knee joint while I was kneeling by Col. Strong's body, securing his valuables. I got another ball on my arm and two on my sword in my hand, so you see I have cause to thank God that he has protected me in this great battle.

The Miller Cornfield at the Antietam battlefield. Howard Carroll of the 105th New York and Henry Strong of the 6th Louisiana fought over this ground. (Brian MacDomhnaill)

Ring's experience bears testament to the storm of fire that engulfed the Miller Cornfield and its environs. For Henry Strong there would be no chance of recovery; Lieutenant Ring later reflected that he had been 'killed while bravely leading his men in the charge.'[62]

The fighting still had many hours to rage. As the battle teetered back and forth across Henry Strong's body, one Union officer picked up one of the Colonel's gloves, waving it triumphantly above his head. Regiment after regiment of Yankees and Rebels were sucked in, chewed up and spat out of the meat-grinder that was the Miller Farm and Cornfield that day. The carnage also spread to the centre and Confederate right flank; only the coming of night brought an end to the bloodiest day in the history of the United States.

The 18 September saw both sides face each other across the charnel house that was the previous day's battlefield, but there was to be no further fighting. Robert E. Lee pulled his Confederate forces back into Virginia, bringing the Maryland Campaign to a close and ending the South's first invasion of Northern territory.

Although Henry Strong had breathed his last on the field, the prospects for Howard Carroll at first appeared bright. His wound did not appear mortal, and it was decided that he should be sent to Washington to aid his recuperation. However, the Dubliner was forced to endure an arduous journey by horse-drawn ambulance to the capital, a distance of well over 100km. Along the way the wound in his leg was aggravated, eventually becoming inflamed. What had initially seemed a non-life threatening injury now caused a fever, from which Howard Carroll would never recover. On 29 September 1862, twelve days after Antietam, the Colonel of the 105th New York Infantry died, adding yet another name to the seemingly endless list of dead.[63]

Union General Alpheus S. Williams rode over the Miller Farm and Cornfield two days after the conclusion of the battle. Although many of the dead and wounded had already been removed, Williams was particularly struck by the number of dead horses. One in particular caught his eye: 'One beautiful milk-white animal had died in so graceful

'One beautiful milk-white animal had died in so graceful a position that I wished for its photograph.' Alexander Gardner's photograph from Antietam is almost certainly the mount of Colonel Henry Strong, 6th Louisiana Infantry. (Library of Congress)

a position that I wished for its photograph. Its legs were doubled under and its arched neck gracefully turned to one side, as if looking back to the ball-hole in its side. Until you got to it, it was hard to believe the horse was dead.' Photographer Alexander Gardner agreed. Gardner would soon be at Antietam taking photographs of the battlefield that would send shockwaves through the North, exposing those at home to real images of the dead for the first time. One of his compositions, probably taken on 20 September, was entitled 'Dead: Horse of a Confederate Colonel; both killed at the Battle of Antietam.' Painstaking research by William A. Frassanito, over 100 years after the conclusion of the war, has revealed that the horse in question is in all probability the mount of none other than Colonel Henry Strong, 6th Louisiana Infantry.[64]

The Battle of Antietam on 17 September 1862 was the bloodiest day in American history. These Confederate soldiers fell near the Dunker Church during the fighting. (Library of Congress)

Howard Carroll's death in Washington was followed by his burial in Rural Cemetery, Albany, New York, where he lies in Section 33, Lot 2. Henry Strong lay where he had fallen until the day after the battle, when a truce allowed some of his men to hastily bury his remains. The Bowie List, published in 1869, recorded the burial places of Confederates who had died at the battles of South Mountain, Monocacy and Antietam. The entry for Henry Strong reads simply: 'In the hollow south of Dunkard Church, 75 steps and 10 feet east of a walnut stump towards the pike.'[65]

Outside the Irish-born officers and generals who served in ethnic Irish regiments or had well-known Fenian connections, few of these men remain well-known to us today. Dozens of Irishmen led regiments into battle on both sides of the conflict – there were twenty-five Irish Colonels who commanded regiments from the state of New York alone, while 11 Irish – born men became Confederate Colonels. Howard Carroll's service in the 105th New York also reflects the fact that the majority of Irishmen who served in the Civil War, regardless of the colour of their uniform, did so in non-ethnic Irish regiments. In many respects it is only through looking at the men in non-green flag units that the majority experience of Irish soldiers in the American Civil War can be fully understood. Howard Carroll and Henry Strong had both left Ireland and made a success of their new lives in the United States. The choices they made about where to live once they arrived on the other side of the Atlantic played a key role in determining their allegiances during the Civil War. It was perhaps this factor more than any other that set them on the path to confrontation at Antietam, where they would receive their death wounds within yards of each other on the Miller Farm.[66]

Slaughter in Saunders' Field

The battlefields of the American Civil War were places of unimaginable carnage. Contemporary tactics demanded that attacking units form a line of battle – usually consisting of a regiment forming two ranks – with the men advancing shoulder to shoulder. While they did so a devastating stream of death was thrown at them by their opponents in an effort to force them back. At long range, artillery would fire at oncoming soldiers with solid shot and explosive shells, projectiles which could mangle or even vaporise men. As the attack closed in, the big guns changed to ammunition such as canister, a metal container filled with dozens of iron balls. This container disintegrated once fired, causing the balls to scatter like a giant shotgun blast, literally mowing down anyone in its path. Added to this was the small arms fire of enemy infantry. Increasingly during the war men were armed with the muzzle-loading rifled-musket, a gun which fired a conical minié ball further and more accurately than its smoothbore predecessor. At closer range these bullets could blow right through a front rank soldier and take down the man behind him.

In the face of such conditions, as the war progressed both Yankee and Rebel infantry learned to fortify their positions as soon as they arrived on the battlefield. Veterans realised that even a hastily prepared hole scratched in the earth or a rudimentary timber barricade could mean the difference between life and death. However, as defenders began to protect themselves in entrenchments and behind breastworks, the task of those attacking them became even more daunting. This deadly combination of fortified defenders and murderously efficient weaponry created conditions where large numbers of men could be wiped out in a matter of moments. It was into just such a perfect storm of death that the Irishmen of the 9th Massachusetts Infantry found themselves ordered on 5 May 1864, a day that none of those who endured it would ever forget.

The 9th Massachusetts Infantry do not enjoy the renown that is the lot of some other ethnic Irish regiments. They did not serve in the Irish Brigade, and did not do their heaviest fighting on famous fields such as Antietam and Gettysburg. Despite this there were few of their countrymen who could claim to have endured more severe tests than the 9th. They owed its origins to the pre-war Columbian Artillery, a Boston militia unit

Officers of the 9th Massachusetts Infantry at religious service in camp near Washington DC. (Library of Congress)

composed of Irishmen. It had been disbanded along with all other militia companies made up of foreigners by the city's Know-Nothing Governor Henry Gardner in 1855. Despite this the company's captain, Thomas Cass, had preserved it as a civil organisation until the outbreak of the Civil War. He then used the Columbian Artillery as the core around which he raised the 9th. Over a thousand Irishmen marched off to war with Cass, now a Colonel, at their head on 25 June 1861.[67]

By 1864 few of that original thousand were left. Colonel Cass was dead, having been mortally wounded at the Battle of Malvern Hill in 1862. Many of his men had also fallen. Those who remained were no strangers to intense combat. The regiment bore the dubious honour of having been the Union unit that had suffered the highest number of casualties at Gaines' Mill on 27 June 1862, Robert E. Lee's first victory at the head of the Confederate Army of Northern Virginia. At that battle the 9th had endured hours of fighting, being among the longest engaged of all Yankee troops. They had sustained a staggering loss of 249 men, eighty-two of whom were killed. Despite this experience, the Irishmen would soon discover that the 1864 campaign would hold equally harrowing ordeals.[68]

The Colonel of the regiment in the spring of 1864 was Patrick Guiney, a native of Parkstown, Co. Tipperary. He and his men formed part of Brigadier-General Charles Griffin's 1st Division of the 5th Army Corps, Army of the Potomac. Lieutenant-General Ulysses S. Grant had recently taken command of all Federal armies, and for the first time he intended to coordinate simultaneous offensives by all Union armies against the South. He was also about to bring a new type of war to the Eastern Theater. Where in previous years campaigns had been characterised by one or two battles followed by periods of inactivity, Grant realised that to exploit the North's superior manpower the Union had to keep constant pressure on the Rebels. From now on, win or lose, there would be no retreat. The fighting would be constant and brutal, as the Yankees sought to grind down their numerically weaker opponent.

The 1864 campaign commenced with the Army of the Potomac crossing the Rapidan River on 4 May. The initial part of the advance was through an inhospitable area known as the Wilderness. This was not a location Ulysses S. Grant would have chosen to fight Robert E. Lee. The region had gained its name as a result of the heavily wooded terrain and thick undergrowth that characterised it. It made command and control almost impossible, and worse still it negated the advantage in numbers which the Union Army enjoyed. Grant had hoped his troops could clear this obstacle before the Rebels struck, but on 5 May Lee successfully managed to barrel elements of his Army of Northern Virginia into the Union 5th Corps before the Yankees could extricate themselves. The Battle of the Wilderness had commenced.[69]

Brigadier-General Charles Griffin and the rest of the 5th Corps had not expected to encounter Rebels anywhere near the Orange Turnpike along which they were positioned on 5 May. It quickly became clear that the enemy was on top of them when skirmish fire erupted along

Prior to reaching Saunders' Field the 9th Massachusetts advanced through terrain like this, which gave the area its name, the Wilderness. The undergrowth hampered efforts to locate and bury the dead, and human remains lay scattered throughout the area. (Library of Congress)

Griffin's line. With the Corps spread out, Griffin was ordered to take his 1st Division forward to counter the enemy advance, and buy time for the rest of the divisions to form up. He faced west along the Turnpike, placing two brigades in front on either side of the road, with a third, Sweitzer's, in support. Among the regiments that formed part of this support was the 9th Massachusetts Infantry.[70]

As Griffin's men advanced they encountered the main Confederate line in the vicinity of Saunders' Field. This was one of the few cleared areas in the Wilderness, some 400 yards deep and 800 yards wide with the Turnpike running roughly through its centre. With the Rebels arrayed in the treeline along the field's western edge, the Yankees would have to expose themselves to merciless fire as they crossed the exposed ground – the conditions were perfect to create one of the worst charnel houses seen during the Civil War.[71]

Griffin's first two brigades pushed into the field, with predictable results. As they crossed the open ground one soldier looked about to see 'killed and wounded men plunging to the ground'. Survivors remembered that 'with the rattle of the musketry was interspersed the booming of the cannon stationed on the road'. Another Northerner was horrified to see that his regiment had 'melted away like snow. Men disappeared as if the earth had swallowed them.' Battery D of the 1st New York Light Artillery were sent racing into the field in an effort to assist their infantry counterparts, as yet more troops were committed to the fray. The exposed clearing proved to be no place for artillery. When the Union attacks were driven back the Confederates stormed forward and amid ferocious hand to hand combat captured the guns. As the fighting continued to rage back and forth, Griffin called on his reserve brigade to enter the meat grinder. For the 9th Massachusetts, the moment of truth had arrived.[72]

Daniel MacNamara remembered that the regiment plunged through the trees and scrub when they 'suddenly broke into a valley-like clearing of several acres'. This was Saunders' Field. Here the 9th were confronted by

Confederate defences at the edge of Saunders' Field, the Wilderness. It was against
Rebels along this treeline that the 9th Massachusetts advanced on 5 May 1864.

the captured artillery pieces. The guns were now in no man's land, but the Rebels had decked them out in Southern flags. The Irish did not realise that the area around the guns was a killing zone, swept by Confederate fire. Indeed the flags were probably placed on the guns by the Rebels in the hope that a Union force would be drawn out to try and capture them.[73]

The regiment dashed into the field with a yell in an attempt to recapture their guns. Colonel Guiney was one of the first to go down. A bullet smashed into his face, carrying away his left eye and scarring him for life. Lieutenant-Colonel Patrick Hanley took over command, but within seconds officers and men were falling everywhere. Daniel MacNamara recalled that the men endured 'a terrific fire from a large body of infantry concealed in the woods on front and flank, under which, if repeated, not a man would have been left.' After only a matter of minutes, the 9th Massachusetts had been utterly decimated. With no support on either flank, Hanley had no option but to order his stunned men back to the cover of the trees. Incredibly, the hell they had experienced in Saunders' Field had been so brief that their brigade commander, Jacob Sweitzer, failed to notice that they had even attempted to enter the clearing. Sweitzer rushed up to confront Hanley and demanded to know why he didn't take his regiment in. An incredulous Hanley replied 'We have been in, and just come out!' Unmoved, Sweitzer ordered him to push the 9th back into Saunders' Field. Hanley turned to the survivors, stating simply 'Fall in, Ninth!'[74]

Hanley might have been excused for pointing out to his commanding officer that the absence of his regimental Colonel Patrick Guiney and many of the rest of the Massachusetts Irishmen was proof enough that the 9th had already been engaged. Nevertheless, he formed the men up in line of battle to prepare to enter the killing ground once more. Fortunately, the division commander Brigadier-General Griffin appeared to have retained a better grasp of the situation than Colonel Sweitzer. He saw the shattered regiment preparing to go in again, and swiftly sent a staff officer to countermand the order; their fighting was finished for the day.[75]

The Battle of the Wilderness raged into 6 May, but the Irishmen would not again face serious fighting. The day after the battle, Colonel Sweitzer sought out Hanley to apologise for his actions, stating that he did not realise the regiment had been engaged and taken such casualties.

There was more bloodshed to come in the weeks ahead as what became known as the Overland Campaign continued, but for this group of men the end was in sight. The 9th Massachusetts completed its three-year term of service and mustered out for their return to Boston on 21 June 1864. Had it not been for the Wilderness, far more of them would have made that long awaited trip home.[76]

Just how many men was it possible to lose in such a short period of time? A full day of hard fighting at Gaines' Mill in 1862 had cost the regiment 249 casualties. In contrast, the Wilderness had seen a fewer number of men engaged so briefly that even their own brigade commander missed it. Given the circumstances, the butcher's bill was truly staggering. A total of 150 officers and men had been killed and wounded. The experience of the 9th Massachusetts in Saunders' Field is a sobering example of what the weaponry of the 1860s was capable of doing to massed ranks of men caught in the open.

For many in the Irish community of Boston the repercussions of those few minutes would last for decades. Some of the wounded were maimed for life, both physically and psychologically. The families of the slain were forced to cope without husbands, fathers and brothers, creating an on-going emotional and financial hole that was often never filled. It can be difficult to look at casualties such as those sustained by the 9th Massachusetts as more than a number, but veteran and historian of the regiment Daniel MacNamara did not view them this way. When he compiled his history of the regiment in 1899 he was careful to name each of the men who was killed or wounded in those few minutes. His list brings home the reality of what Saunders' Field really meant.

Killed and Mortally Wounded[77]

Captains James W. MacNamara, William A. Phelan; 1st Lieutenant Nicholas C. Flaherty; 2nd Lieutenant Charles B. McGinniskin.

COMPANY A
Sergeant Thomas Fitzgerald; Corporal Paul McCluskey (died of wounds 15 July 1864, at Andersonville, Ga); Privates John Coffee, Timothy Rahilly.

COMPANY B
Privates Martin Sheehan, John Ferris, John Reagan, James Ward.

COMPANY C
Privates Michael Dolan, John Flanagan, Edward Pettie, Erasmus D. Marden or Madden.

COMPANY D
Corporals James I. Healey, James McCann; Private James Walsh.

COMPANY E
Corporal Richard Condon; Privates James Mullooney, Thomas Murphy, Bernard Conway (died of wounds 9 July 1864, at Philadelphia).

COMPANY F
Private Patrick Shea, died of wounds 31 May 1864.

COMPANY G
Privates John Connors, Jedediah Bumpus, Richard Furfey, Peter Hughes, Patrick Mulloy, George L. Green (died of wounds 12 May 1864).

COMPANY H
Privates Francis Finnerty, William Peachy, James O'Connell (died of wounds in prison 7 October 1864).

COMPANY I
Corporal Bernard Hayes; Privates Stephen Blake, William Gillis (died of wounds 5 May 1864), Michael Garrity (died of wounds 17 June 1864), Lawrence Mathews (died of wounds 5 May 1864), Thomas Hackett.

COMPANY K
Sergeant James Hayes (died of wounds 5 May 1864); Privates Michael Connell, Joseph Flynn, Patrick Kelleher, William Schmidt.

List of Wounded

Colonel Patrick R. Guiney; Captains Timothy O'Leary, Timothy Burke; Lieutenants John F. Doherty, Bernard F. Finan, Patrick. Murphy, Joseph Murphy, William A. Plunkett.

COMPANY A
Bartholomew Kelleher, Daniel Mullane, Donald Ross, John McLaughlin, Daniel Kenney Jr, John Moakler, John O'Donnell, Patrick Gallagher, William C. Gardner, Michael Grifffin, James Hickey, Thomas McMahon, Jeremiah Ninan, Peter Smith, David Zeigler, John Weber.

COMPANY B
Patrick Brickley, James Remick, Bernard Lane, Joseph Brown, Joseph Brennan, Henry B. O'Neil, Peter Schofield.

COMPANY C
James McCarthy, Daniel Walsh, Daniel Martin, James Murray, Maurice O'Donnell, William Craig, Henry Flannagan, John Kelleher, Anthony McTighe.

COMPANY D
Edward C. Scott, Thomas Collins, William Cleaveland, John Haggerty, Thomas Keenan or Kerivan, Thomas Kinlan or Kiflan, William McDermott.

COMPANY E
John Halloren, Samuel Smith, Daniel Carney, Francis Hewitt, Daniel O'Connor, James Robinson, Timothy Ryan, John Danahy or Donahue, Daniel Buckley, James Butcher.

COMPANY F
Michael W. Boyle, Thomas Fallon, Edward Geigle, James McLaughlin, Robert Cashin, William Jordan, James Leslie.

COMPANY G
William H. Armstrong, Thomas Hackett, Thomas B. Brigham, Maurice Sullivan, Thomas Conboy, Lawrence Cassidy, James Lanagan, Martin Lydon, Thomas Dineen, Walter Walsh, Peter McQueeny, Oscar Ola.

COMPANY H
Malachi Curley, Thomas Mullen, John Shea, John Melvin, John Holmes, Henry Young, John Foley, James J. Rox, John J. Ford, Michael Finnerty.

COMPANY I

Jeremiah Cronin, Patrick Carroll, William Carroll, Thomas Green, Patrick Herlihy, John Quinn, Cornelius Dacey, Thomas J. Lewellen, Henry Coy, John Gallagher, John Palmer, Thomas Sheridan, James McNeil, Zenas A. Butterfield.

COMPANY K

John J. Breen, Patrick Cunningham, Michael Barry, Justin Eberhardt, John McGowan, Mathias Naphut.

Blood on the banner

The Congressional Medal of Honor is the United States' highest military award. It was created on 21 December 1861 to recognise gallantry and intrepidity at the risk of life and above and beyond the call of duty. It started its history as a naval award, and was initially restricted to enlisted personnel in the United States Navy and marines. An army Medal of Honor was created on 12 July 1862, and at first was likewise restricted to enlisted men. From 3 March 1863 army officers were also entitled to receive the award, although naval officers would remain ineligible until 1915.[78]

No foreign nationality has received the Medal of Honor on more occasions than the Irish. In the American Civil War a total of 146 recipients have been identified as Irish-born, representing almost 10 per cent of the total from the conflict. Although the history of Irish contributions to the war tends to focus on ethnic regiments such as those of the Irish Brigade, the reality was that the vast majority of Irishmen served in non-Irish units. One of the few ways of visualising this contribution is by looking at those men who received the medal. Of the 146 Irishmen, fewer than twenty served in what might be called 'Irish' regiments. In contrast, a total of fifty of the 327 naval recipients during the Civil War were born in Ireland, although virtually no analysis has been carried out on the Irish contribution to the US Navy between 1861 and 1865.[79]

The types of actions that led to the award of the Medal of Honor could vary widely, from the capture of an enemy flag, to the rescue of wounded comrades or the storming of enemy positions. In the majority of cases it required an act of extreme heroism, and often one of extreme sacrifice. One of the most famous Irish recipients of the award was Sergeant Thomas Plunkett of the 21st Massachusetts Infantry. Few men paid as high a price as this Irishman did for his bravery.

Thomas Plunkett was a bootmaker who lived in West Boylston, Massachusetts before the outbreak of the war. His family had emigrated from Co. Mayo in the mid-1840s, when Thomas was still a boy. He enlisted in Company E of the 21st Massachusetts at the age of twenty-one, and mustered into Union service on 23 August 1861. The regiment was overwhelmingly American, with over 600 of the 829 enlisted men born in the United States; Thomas was one of only eighty-seven soldiers from Ireland. He soon marked himself out as an exemplary soldier, quickly winning promotion to Sergeant. Plunkett proved this at the Battle of Chantilly on 1 September 1862, when he earned the admiration of his comrades for attempting to rescue a wounded friend. Leaving his musket behind, he moved into a set of woods occupied by the enemy in an effort to bring the man out. Although he was unable to find his friend, along the way he encountered a Confederate soldier standing guard by a tree. He promptly set upon the Rebel, wrenching away his gun and dragging him back to Union lines as a prisoner.[80]

The act for which Plunkett won lasting fame in Massachusetts came with the Battle of Fredericksburg, Virginia, fought on 13 December 1862. The engagement resulted from the efforts of the Union Army of the Potomac to force a crossing of the Rappahannock River at Fredericksburg, defended by the Confederate Army of Northern Virginia. Although the Federal commander Major-General Ambrose Burnside successfully took the town of Fredericksburg on the south bank, he proceeded to throw his army piecemeal against the strongly fortified Rebel positions on the heights beyond. In what became one of the most lop-sided battles of the war, brigade after brigade of Yankees were shattered against the Rebel line in a series of disastrous assaults. What became the most famous portion of the Confederate line was located behind a stone wall at the base of Marye's Heights. Among the units that were sacrificed against this position were the Irish Brigade; another was the brigade of Brigadier-General Edward Ferrero, which included the 21st Massachusetts and Thomas Plunkett.

Ferrero's men had spent much of the 13th watching the Irish Brigade and others dash themselves against the stone wall with no result aside from sustaining tremendous casualties. Their turn finally came a little after 2 p.m., when Thomas Plunkett and his comrades were ordered to advance. Marching up Fredericksburg's Prussia Street they moved out into the open ground beyond, negotiating a mill race before preparing for the final assault. They quickly came under murderous Rebel artillery fire; as they formed up the head of one 21st Massachusetts soldier was thrown from his shoulders by a cannonball, causing a 'horrid red fountain' to spout from his neck. This set the tone for what lay ahead.[81]

As the brigade advanced the fire intensified, and some of the panicked soldiers grew close to tears. One cried out 'Oh, dear! they'll kill every one of us; not a damned one of us will be left to tell the story!' Survivors from previous failed assaults streamed back through their ranks, shouting 'Don't go up there; the day is lost!' But the brigade pressed on. One of the 21st Massachusetts men described how the regiment advanced through a 'hell of countless projectiles which shrieked, burst, and hissed through the air, or tore the ground again and again'. The colors of the 21st became a major focus of Rebel fire; Color Corporal Elbridge C. Barr of Company C, carrying the state colors, and Color Sergeant Joseph H. Collins of Company A, who held aloft the national colors, both fell mortally wounded. Up to this point Thomas Plunkett had been positioned at the rear of the regiment, with orders to prevent any of the

The stone wall defended by the Confederates at Marye's Heights, Fredericksburg. This was the wall charged by Thomas Plunkett and the 21st Massachusetts, as well as the Irish Brigade. This photo was taken after the wall's capture a few months later as part of the Battle of Chancellorsville. (Library of Congress)

men from falling back. When he saw Collins go down with the national flag, he threw away his gun and sprang forward to take up the colors, leading the Massachusetts men forwards towards the stone wall.[82]

Finally, having advanced to within 200 yards of the enemy position, the 21st halted to unleash its first volley at the Confederates. Now a valued target himself, Plunkett had a near miss when a bullet pierced his cap. He was fortunate on that occasion, but Thomas's luck was about to run out.

A shell flew towards the exposed color party and exploded in front of the Irish sergeant. Three of the men around him were killed, and a shrapnel fragment spun into Plunkett's right arm near the shoulder, leaving the limb dangling by a strip of flesh. The deadly piece of shell travelled on towards his chest, where it collided with a book that Thomas had picked up in Fredericksburg earlier in the day. The book saved his life, but the shrapnel was not done with him. The red hot metal journeyed on, smashing into his left wrist and gouging out another terrible wound. Incredibly, Plunkett didn't go down. Through what must have been superhuman effort he managed to keep the banner aloft, shouting out 'Don't let it fall boys, don't let it fall!' As he sank to the ground the color was literally soaked in what Lieutenant-Colonel Clark of the regiment assumed was the Irishman's 'life blood'. Bradley R. Olney of Company H stepped in to relive Plunkett of his charge, and eventually Thomas was carried towards the rear where he was stretchered to a temporary hospital in Fredericksburg.[83]

Thomas Plunkett's life hung in the balance as he was carried into the town. He was exceptionally fortunate to have by his side one of the most famous nurses the American Civil War produced. Clara Barton, the future founder of the American Red Cross, had a special affinity with the 21st Massachusetts and stayed with the Irishman as his mangled body was operated upon. The surgeons had to remove what remained of both of his arms, pare back the ragged remains of the limb bones, and sew up what remained. He somehow managed to survive; when she was later shown the national colors that Plunkett had carried, Clara Barton observed that his blood 'literally obliterated the stripes'.[84]

By the 25 December Thomas had improved enough to be moved from the front. At noon he and other wounded members of the 21st were carried to the railway station en-route to Acquia Creek and ultimately Washington. On the way to the train they were greeted by the survivors of their regiment, who had turned out to provide an escort to Plunkett and the others. The soldiers stood to attention at 'present arms' as the stretchers were carried past. For Thomas the long road to recovery had begun.[85]

Sergeant Thomas Plunkett of the 21st Massachusetts Infantry poses with the regimental colors. While carrying the flag at Fredericksburg in 1862 he was so severely wounded that his blood 'literally obliterated the stripes'. (The Florida Center for Instructional Technology)

Plunkett would never forget the kindness that Clara Barton had shown him at Fredericksburg, and he would soon have need of her assistance once again. In Washington he had been cared for in the Armory Square Hospital, and eventually he recuperated enough to travel home to Massachusetts. His brother Francis journeyed to the capital to help his brother make the trip, but found that the army would not release the soldier. Francis was further frustrated as his efforts to resolve the situation with the War Department fell on deaf ears. Clara was then in Washington,

Clara Barton, who nursed Thomas Plunkett in Fredericksburg, and without whose assistance he may well have died. (Library of Congress)

and when informed of the situation she led the Plunketts straight to the Capitol Building to see Massachusetts Senator Henry Wilson. When Wilson emerged to greet them in the waiting room, the indomitable nurse said 'Mr. Wilson, allow me to introduce you to Sergeant Plunkett of the Massachusetts Twenty-first.' The politician instinctively extended his hand to the Irishman, which of course Thomas could not shake. Clara interceded 'You will pardon the Sergeant for not offering you a hand, he has none.' Shocked, Wilson exclaimed 'No hands! No hands! My God; where are they?' The situation was explained to the Senator, who was clearly shocked at the physical price Plunkett had paid on the field of battle. He promised to take his predicament up with the War Department straight away. By the following day everything had been resolved, and Thomas and his brother were free to travel home to Massachusetts.[86]

Thomas Plunkett had lost both his arms while clinging to the national flag. That his sacrifice was a powerful allegory for the efforts of the North to defend the Union was evident to all. His fame quickly spread, and even his movements were now recorded with interest. The *Springfield Republican* informed its readers on 1 April 1863 of Plunkett's progress towards home, letting them know that he had by that point reached New York, where he was staying at the New England rooms. While in New York Thomas began to experience the special attention that was to become the norm – he was taken to visit both the Stock Exchange and the Chamber of Commerce, where he received gifts and expressions of sympathy. Meanwhile a subscription had been proposed to raise money for artificial arms, and eventually the businessmen of New York and Boston would contribute $7,000 to assist the wounded man. In addition the Legislature of Massachusetts voted him a gratuity of $100 a year, and when Thomas was finally discharged from military service on 9 March 1864 he was also granted a full pension.[87]

Life would never be the same for Plunkett after Fredericksburg, but he did his best to have as normal an existence as possible. He married on 26 November 1863, and went on to have two sons. He also returned to the workforce, gaining a position as a messenger in the State House in Boston, where he would work for fifteen years. Although his disability meant that he needed to have an attendant with him for much of the time, it is clear that he did his utmost not to let his injuries hold him back. One report explained that there 'were many things he could do that seemed inexplicable to those around him. For instance, he could drive the fiercest of horses, and often enjoyed an airing upon the road. With the reins over his shoulders, he was able to guide and control the animal in a manner that would do credit to the most expert horseman.' He also proved extremely astute with money, amassing property estimated at between $20,000 and $25,000 in value.

Unsurprisingly Thomas remained close to his wartime comrades. When the 21st Massachusetts returned from the conflict on 1 February 1864, it was Plunkett who marched beside the colors during the regiment's reception in Worcester. He also became an active participant in the Union veterans' organisation, the Grand Army of the Republic, where he was a member of George H. Ward Post 10.[88]

Thomas Plunkett's fulfilling post-war life was brought to a close on 10 March 1885, when he died as a result of illness at the age of forty-four. He was buried in Hope Cemetery, Worcester. Thomas's fame had endured; sketches of his body lying in state were produced for publications such as *Leslie's Weekly*, and his continuing popularity was exemplified on 22 November 1895 when a huge crowd attended the unveiling of a portrait of Thomas by J. Madison Stone at Mechanic's Hall, Boston.[89]

Perhaps the greatest honour Thomas Plunkett received following the war came on 30 March 1866, when he was awarded the Congressional Medal of Honor. His citation was brief and to the point, as was typical of the time. It read: 'Seized the colors of his regiment, the color bearer having been shot down, and bore them to the front where both his arms were carried off by a shell.'

There is little question that the early financial support Thomas received and the assistance of the grateful people of Massachusetts helped him to

The wound that Private John Quinn of Company I received at the Battle of the Wilderness ended his time as a soldier. He received this 'Honor to the Brave' certificate which lists the battles in which he fought with the 9th Massachusetts. Having survived the bloodbath in Saunder's Field, Quinn went on to live until 1892. (Joe Maghe Collection)

overcome both the physical and psychological impact of the horrendous injuries he had suffered. Unfortunately his story was far from typical of all Irish-born Medal of Honor recipients. The Mayo emigrant retains his place as a revered figure in Massachusetts history. The Massachusetts State House now houses the national color of the 21st Massachusetts Infantry, which even today remains covered in the blood of Thomas Plunkett.[90]

Death of a General

It was the early afternoon of 30 November 1864 when Brigadier-General Daniel C. Govan stood with his division commander, Major-General

Patrick Cleburne, on Winstead Hill, just outside Franklin, Tennessee. As they prepared their troops for the attack, Govan scanned the fortified Federal positions around the town, and the exposed plain over which the Army of Tennessee was to advance. The prospects for success seemed bleak. Just before the advance was sounded, Govan turned to Cleburne, whom he thought looked despondent, and remarked, 'Well General, there will not be many of us that will get back to Arkansas.' Cleburne turned to his fellow Helena resident, replying: 'Well Govan, if we are to die, let us die like men.'[91]

There are surely few Irishmen who enjoy such differential recognition between their native and adoptive countries as Patrick Ronayne Cleburne. Such is his standing in the United States that he has counties named for him in Alabama and Arkansas, a Confederate cemetery bears his name in Georgia, and the city of around 30,000 people in Cleburne, Texas, was titled in his honour. In contrast he is virtually unheard of both in Ireland and in his native county of Cork, save for a modest plaque erected on the house of his birth in 1994 by visiting American admirers. That house is Bride Park Cottage, Killumney, where Cleburne was born on 16 March 1828, the third of four children. Patrick was baptised at St Mary's church, the local Church of Ireland establishment, in Athnowen Parish. His father Joseph was a doctor who was a contract surgeon at the barracks and gunpowder mill in Ballincollig, a position that kept the family in some comfort. Patrick's mother Mary Anne died when he was just 18 months old, but the young boy would not have long to wait for the return of a maternal figure as his father married Isabella Stuart in 1830, and a half-sister and three half-brothers followed.[92]

By 1836 the upwardly mobile Joseph Cleburne decided to divide his time between medicine and farming, and he took on the lease of nearby Grange manor house and its 206 acres. Life was good during those years, but the Cleburne's fortunes were soon to take a turn for the worse. Dr Joseph Cleburne died of typhus on 27 November 1843, immediately placing the family in a precarious financial position. The teenage Patrick moved to Mallow in 1844, where he became an apprentice to the local surgeon Dr Thomas Justice, in the hope of following his father into medicine.[93]

The turning point in Patrick Cleburne's life came in 1846, when he failed the entrance exam to the Apothecaries' Hall, Dublin. This rejection not only prevented him from following in his father's footsteps, it also left him deeply ashamed. Unable to face his family in Cork, he instead made the rash decision to enlist as a private in the 41st Foot. It was a decision he regretted. Choosing not to let anyone know of what had become of him, he had been in the ranks for over a year before an officer who knew his family recognised him and his relatives learned of his whereabouts. It was now 1847, and the officer had Patrick transferred to his own company. He proved to be a good soldier, and by 1849 he had been promoted to corporal. The death of his father and the disaster of the Famine had seriously impacted on the viability of the Cleburne lands at Grange, and the majority of Patrick's siblings decided to emigrate. Patrick was of a like mind, but needed to find a way out of the army. He finally bought his discharge from the British Army for £20 in September 1849. Wasting no time, the future general landed in New Orleans on Christmas Day the same year.[94]

The outbreak of the American Civil War in 1861 found a man with much improved fortunes from the twenty-one-year-old who had departed from Queenstown over a decade earlier. Patrick Cleburne had found a new life on the Mississippi River, where he was the joint owner of a drug store in Helena, Arkansas. As a respected and popular member of the local community and an active Democrat, he had become fully accepted by his adopted homeland, and in return Cleburne was fully committed to Arkansas. His wartime career began as captain of the local Yell Rifles, which soon joined a number of other companies to form the 1st Arkansas Infantry. The Corkman was elected colonel of the regiment upon its creation. By the end of 1861 he had already commanded a brigade, and he received official notification that he had been promoted to general on 4 March 1862. Brigadier-General Cleburne was quickly marking himself out as a brilliant fighter and leader of men, and over the course of the next two years his star would continue to rise.[95]

By the autumn of 1864 Patrick Ronayne Cleburne, now a major-general, had built a reputation as the finest Confederate division commander in the Western Theater. He had achieved the highest-rank of any Irishman on either side during the American Civil War, along the way receiving the thanks of the Confederate Congress for saving the Army of Tennessee at Ringgold Gap in 1863. There were many of his contemporaries who felt he should have commanded at a higher level. One of the main reasons he did not was an extraordinary proposal he submitted for the consideration of the Confederate government on 2 January 1864. The Irishman realised that the war was being lost by the Confederacy, and that the superior manpower and resources of the North were taking their toll. He felt there was only one logical course of action:

> … immediately commence training a large reserve of the most courageous of our slaves, and further that we guarantee freedom within a reasonable time to every slave in the South who shall remain true to the Confederacy in this war. As between the loss of independence and the loss of slavery, we assume that every patriot will freely give up the latter-give up the negro slaves rather than be a slave himself.[96]

Cleburne had miscalculated. Although some of his army comrades supported his proposal, others were incensed. The idea of arming Negros was abhorrent to many in the South, and the document was ordered suppressed. Indeed its existence did not come to light until

Major-General Patrick Ronayne Cleburne, CSA. Cleburne was the highest ranking Irish-born General on either side during the American Civil War. He was killed in action at the Battle of Franklin, Tennessee, on 30 November 1864. (Library of Congress)

a number of years after the war's conclusion. The Irishman accepted the decision without comment, although the continued decline in the Confederacy's fortunes he predicted came to pass. The key city of Atlanta fell to William Tecumseh Sherman and his Union troops on 2 September 1864, losing for the South not only a vital rail hub but also striking a devastating psychological blow. As Sherman's imperious soldiers marched east towards the sea, the commander of the Rebels, John Bell Hood, decided to strike west for Tennessee in an effort to draw the main Yankee Army off. Although this ploy failed, Hood continued his march away from Sherman, until on 30 November Cleburne and the Army of Tennessee found themselves outside Franklin. Despite the town's daunting defences and the fact that the 33,000 Confederates only outnumbered their entrenched enemy by around 3,000 men, Hood ordered a full-scale attack; Patrick Cleburne and his division were among those who moved off Winstead Hill towards the town.

Today the Confederate assault against the Union centre at the Battle of Gettysburg, known as 'Pickett's Charge', has become the iconic symbol of a desperate, gallant and ultimately futile Southern effort to break their enemy's line. However, the much less well-known Rebel assault at Franklin was both larger and bloodier. The heaviest fighting took place in a period of two hours, with the general engagement lasting five. At the end of the savage struggle, much of which was at close quarters, the Union still held the town. Although the Yankees pulled out towards Nashville that night, there was no doubting that this had been a crushing blow to the Confederate Army of Tennessee. Daniel Govan had remarked that Cleburne had appeared despondent before the battle, and the casualty figures would have confirmed the Irishman's worst fears. By the time the guns fell silent some 8,500 Union and Confederate soldiers had become casualties. Among the Southern losses were no fewer than six generals, four of whom were laid out together the following morning on the porch of nearby Carnton House. Included in their number was Patrick Ronayne Cleburne.[97]

But what of Cleburne's final moments? Captain Irving Buck, who had been the Irishman's adjutant but had missed Franklin due to earlier wounds, was determined to find out. When the war ended he corresponded with former members of the Army of Tennessee, collecting and publishing as much information as he could about his old chief's demise. One of the accounts he received was from Daniel Govan, who had noted Cleburne's mood before the attack. He described the advance:

> After receiving his final orders we were directed to advance, which was about 2 o'clock in the afternoon. We had to advance across an old open common, subjected to the heavy fire of the Federal forces. We met the enemy in a short space of time and carried the first line commanded by General Wagner [this force had been caught holding an exposed position well in advance of the main Union line]. When that line was broken, General Cleburne's object seemed to be to run into the rear line with the fleeing Federal's from Wagner's division. About that time General Cleburne's horse was killed. His courier brought him another, and as he was in the act of mounting, this horse was killed. He then disappeared in the smoke of battle, and that was the last time I ever saw him alive. I spoke to his aide-de-camp, Mangum, and told him I was sure the General would be killed, as I did not see how he could escape with his life under such terrific fire, and as he never again appeared in the lines, confirmed my opinion that he was dead.[98]

It appears that when Cleburne's first horse was killed the momentum of the dying animal carried the Corkman almost as far as the ditch on the outside of the Union entrenchments. The second horse he was mounting had been struck by a cannonball fired from the direction of a Cotton Gin within the Federal lines. At this point the General moved forward on foot, waving his cap and encouraging his men to advance. He only made it some twenty yards before receiving his mortal wound. It seems that Patrick Cleburne decided to charge Franklin's defences accompanied by his fellow countrymen. The 5th Confederate Infantry was largely made up of Irishmen from Memphis and the surrounding area, and served in Cleburne's Division. Charles W. Frazer, who had served with the regiment earlier in the war and later wrote the unit's history, stated that at Franklin, Cleburne 'charged in with it, and died with it.'[99]

His body was found the next morning by John McQuade of Vicksburg:

> I and two others were the first to discover his dead body at early dawn the next morning. He was about 40 or 50 yards from the works. He lay flat upon his back as if asleep, his military cap partly over his eye. He had on a new gray uniform, the coat of the sack or blouse pattern. It was unbuttoned and open; the lower part of his vest was unbuttoned and open. He wore a white linen shirt, which was stained with blood on the front part of the left side, or just left of the abdomen. This was the only sign of a wound I saw on him, and I believe it is the only one he had received. I have always been inclined to think that feeling the end was near, he had thus laid himself down to die, or that his body had been carried there during the night. He was in his sock feet, his boots having been stolen. His watch, sword belt and other valuables were all gone, his body having been robbed during the night.[100]

From here Patrick Cleburne was taken in an ambulance to Carnton House. Earlier in the campaign the Army of Tennessee had passed a cemetery at St John's church in Ashwood, Tennessee. At the time Cleburne had remarked that it was 'almost worth dying for, to be buried in such a beautiful spot.' His comments were remembered, and this became his initial burial place. In 1870 he was reinterred in his adopted home of Helena, Arkansas, where he still rests in Maple Hill Cemetery. A heart-breaking postscript to his death played itself out in Mobile, Alabama, on 5 December 1864. News of the fighting in Franklin had reached the city, and newsboys moved onto the streets shouting out the days headline: 'Reports from Tennessee! Cleburne and other generals killed!' Patrick Cleburne had become engaged to Susan Tarleton of Mobile earlier in 1864. Susan was walking in her garden when she heard a newsboy crying out the top story, the first indication she had of her fiancée's death. She promptly fainted.[101]

Cleburne's loss was keenly felt by the Confederacy. He had earned the sobriquet 'Stonewall of the West' as a result of his prowess in battle, and he enjoyed the respect and devotion of his troops. His long-time commander and friend William J. Hardee said of the Irishman that 'history will take up his fame and hand it down to time for exampling, wherever a courage without stain, a manhood without blemish, an integrity that knew no compromise, and a patriotism that withheld no sacrifice, are honoured of mankind.' No less a personage than Robert E. Lee stated that he had 'inherited the intrepidity of his race. In a field of battle he shone like a meteor on a clouded sky!'[102]

Patrick Ronayne Cleburne remains a well-known and much-loved figure in the United States today. The former surgical apprentice who failed his medical entrance exams and ran away to the British Army could not have imagined how his memory would be preserved. His life remains a frequent topic of biographical study; recent years have seen a statue of him erected at the site of his greatest victory – Ringgold Gap, Georgia – and the location of his death in Franklin reclaimed

The statue to Major-General Patrick Cleburne at Ringgold Gap, Georgia. Cleburne's delaying action here saved the Army of Tennessee and earned him the thanks of Confederate Congress. (Brian MacDomhnaill)

The memorial to Major-General Patrick Cleburne near where he fell at Franklin, Tennessee, in November 1864. (Hal Jespersen)

from development and reconstituted as Cleburne Park. His place as the most talented Irish General of the American Civil War is secure, yet his achievements are tempered by the tragedy of his death at the age of only thirty-six. Like thousands of other Irishmen, he did not live to see the war's conclusion.

The last to fall

Major-General George Gordon Meade, the last commander of the Union Army of the Potomac and the victor of Gettysburg, learned in 1865 that monies were being raised for the family of Thomas Smyth, an Irish-born general who had been killed in the final days of the war.

He promptly sent a contribution to the fund and enclosed a letter to the committee who had organised it:

> I am very glad to learn that the friends of the late Brigadier-General Thomas A. Smyth are endeavouring to raise funds for the support of his family. No more patriotic or Christian duty devolves on our people than the care and protection of the widows and orphans of those who have offered up their lives in serving the nation. And this duty becomes the more imperative when the fallen soldier is one who has shed such lustre on his State as General Smyth. General Smyth I knew him very well, and can bear testimony to his high soldierly conduct, his gallantry on the field of battle, and his esteemable and genial qualities as a gentleman … I have always considered his loss a most serious one to the country, and have mourned with sincere sorrow his sudden death, in the prime of life, and when earning such distinction, and I trust, for the honor of Delaware, that ample provision will be made for his family.[103]

It was not every officer who received such praise from a soldier of Meade's standing. Smyth had built a reputation during the war as one of the Army of the Potomac's finest regiment and brigade commanders, along the way winning the admiration of his fellow officers and men alike.

Thomas Alfred Smyth was born to Thomas and Margaret Smyth on Christmas Day, 1832 in Ballyhooly, Co. Cork. His father Thomas was a local farmer, and it is known that his son worked with him on the land after leaving school. Aside from this, there are few details of Thomas's life before his emigration to the United States, but it is thought that he travelled through England and Scotland and stayed for a time in London and Paris before making his way to America. In 1854 the then twenty-

Thomas Alfred Smyth as a Brigadier-General in the Union Army. He died of wounds less than twelve hours before Robert E. Lee surrendered at Appomattox Court House, becoming the last Union General to be killed in the American Civil War. (Library of Congress)

one-year-old Thomas departed Liverpool aboard the *Sardinia*, which arrived in New York on 10 August.[104]

The young man made his first home in Philadelphia, where he developed a trade as a woodcarver and began to build carriages and coaches with his uncle. The same sense of adventure that had seen him travel to England, France and the United States soon settled on the Corkman again. He decided to join William Walker, an American adventurer, on his expedition to Nicaragua in 1855. A civil war had broken out in the Latin American country between the Democratics and Legitimists, and Walker took the opportunity to enter the conflict on the Democratic side. Walker defeated the Legitimist army and effectively took control of Nicaragua, until he was driven out by the forces of neighbouring countries in 1857. The young Irishman seems not to have enjoyed his time as a soldier of fortune, and upon his return to the United States he seldom referred to his time with Walker.[105]

In 1858 Thomas moved to Wilmington, Delaware, the state with which he would be associated for the rest of his life. On 7 July that year he married Amanda M. Pounder, and struck out on his own as a carriage-maker. He maintained his interest in military affairs, serving as an officer in a local militia company, the First National Guards. When the war broke out in 1861 Smyth raised a company in Wilmington for three months' service, but as a result of a delay in the unit's acceptance by Delaware he took it to Philadelphia, where it became a part of the heavily Irish 24th Pennsylvania. The 24th did not see much action during their three months' service, and following their muster out Smyth returned to Delaware to play an integral role in raising the 1st Delaware Infantry, a three-year regiment of which he became major.[106]

1862 saw Major Smyth and the 1st Delaware engaged in major battles such as Antietam and Fredericksburg, which earned the Irishman valuable combat experience. He was promoted to the rank of colonel and command of the regiment on 7 February 1863. His impressive performance at the Battle of Chancellorsville the following May caught the eye of his superior officers, and he was swiftly raised to command of a brigade – Smyth would now face a full test of his battlefield abilities. The task was made all the more daunting given the location of the next engagement – Gettysburg, Pennsylvania. The Corkman's brigade consisted of the 14th Connecticut, 12th New Jersey, 108th New York and his old regiment the 1st Delaware. As part of the 2nd Army Corps Smyth's men were among the troops who faced 'Pickett's Charge' on 3 July, an attack that would become the most famous assault of the American Civil War. During the ferocious artillery bombardment that presaged the Rebel charge, a shell fragment struck Smyth in the head, cutting him on the nose and face. When it was suggested that he might be scarred by the injury, Smyth replied that he was 'willing to sacrifice my nose for the sake of my country.' His men went on to help repel the Confederate attack, along the way capturing a large number of prisoners and no fewer than nine enemy colors.[107]

In March 1864 Colonel Smyth was appointed to the command of the Irish Brigade, and he led the Irish soldiers through the start of the bloody Overland Campaign in the Battles of the Wilderness and Spotsylvania. One witness to the Irish Brigade's charge against the Rebel works at Spotsylvania on 12 May remembered his impression of Smyth:

> … the gallant Colonel Smyth, whose name is already written in letters of gold on the scroll of military fame … Colonel Smyth was born to command and be respected, and when he takes the lead, his valiant men follow in his footsteps, no matter what impending barriers rise up to impede their progress. He is the man for the times, the man for the dangerous sphere where he is now engaged, not rash, but prudent, and firm as granite in time of danger, and for his strategic movements, he cannot be outflanked by older generals on the field.[108]

Smyth returned to his old division at the end of May, but the Irish Brigade would retain a soft spot for the Colonel, who although a strict disciplinarian, was highly regarded as a superb leader. The brigade arranged for a poem to be written in his honour, which was read to him prior to his departure. The verses celebrated both Smyth and the Irish Brigade:

'Tom Smyth', proud Columbia can boast
Of no soldier more loyal or true;
No star from her flag shall be lost,
While she's guarded by heroes like you
We grudge not our blood in her cause,
Nor her young beneath her turf laid;
But we'll fight for her union and laws,
'Tom Smyth', and the Irish Brigade.[109]

Despite the fact that Smyth had been commanding a brigade since Gettysburg, and by the late summer of 1864 was even temporarily taking charge at divisional level, he still had not received promotion to general. This was finally rectified on 1 October 1864, when he achieved the rank of brigadier-general of volunteers. The news was greeted with delight by Smyth's officers and men. Gifts to celebrate his promotion began to flood in from commands old and new. His staff presented him with a set of fine shoulder straps, while his old regiment the 1st Delaware and the 63rd New York, Irish Brigade each purchased him a horse. The Irish Brigade sent an agent to Washington to secure horse fittings, a sword and other accoutrements to a value of $1200. When the men of his brigade, then manning trenches at Petersburg, Virginia, heard the news of the promotion, they raised such prolonged cheers that their Confederate counterparts wondered what the occasion was.[110]

Thomas Smyth's promotion to Brigadier-General did affect one aspect of his wartime life. Smyth was an active Fenian, having been sworn into the brotherhood by John O'Mahony in Wilmington, Delaware. The Fenians were dedicated to furthering the cause of Irish independence from British rule, and hoped after the war to make use of the military experience gained by many of their members to engage in an armed struggle in Ireland. They were organised in groups known as 'circles', which met regularly to discuss Fenian business. Among the most famous was the Army of the Potomac circle. It included many notable Irish officers, and Thomas Smyth at one point served as its president. So influential was Smyth in the movement that in 1864 he was elected to the national central council of five, but he soon found that his duties as a general at the front made it impossible for him to maintain this position. On 31 January 1865 he wrote to John O'Mahony stating that he would not be able to attend the upcoming meeting of the council as he was now temporarily leading a division, and Lieutenant-General Grant had cancelled all leave. He informed O'Mahony that 'it is with reluctance I take this step; but my duty to my country demanded of me to resign a position that I cannot attend to, and perform the most important duty imposed on me as one of the officers of the brotherhood.' Despite his inability to continue in the council, Smyth nonetheless did resolve to continue as 'a working member of the body.'[111]

Thomas Smyth was now free to concentrate completely on events at the front, which were soon to take a decisive turn for the Union cause. On 2 April 1865 Grant ordered a general assault along the lines at Petersburg, Virginia, which finally broke the Rebel defences that had been in place for over nine months. Robert E. Lee and the Army of Northern Virginia abandoned the city on 3 April, an action which also doomed the Confederate capital of Richmond. Lee fled west with his army towards Appomattox, with the Yankees hard on his heels.[112]

On 6 April 1865 Brigadier-General Smyth wrote in his diary: 'orders to march at 5 a.m. and at 6 o'clock to assault the enemy's works.' It was to be his final entry. On the morning of 7 April his brigade was in pursuit of the Rebels in the vicinity of High Bridge, which spanned the Appomattox River. The Confederates were desperately attempting to set fire to the bridge to stall the Federal pursuit, but the 2nd Corps, of which Smyth's brigade was a part, managed to capture the structure substantively intact. This meant that the Union troops could keep up direct pressure on the Rebels, who were trying to reach the town of Farmville, where crucial rations waited for the hungry Army of Northern Virginia.[113]

The General was a commander who led from the front, often exposing himself to enemy fire. A few weeks previously he had been riding with a staff officer along the line when he had been fired on at close range by Rebel pickets. That night some Confederate deserters came into Union lines. One of the men, upon seeing Smyth, exclaimed 'Why you are the very General I shot at this afternoon!' The Rebel explained that the temptation of trying to hit a Union General was too great to resist. The Irishman had been lucky on that occasion, but his tendency to expose himself on the line was soon to have fatal consequences.[114]

Once the Yankees got across High Bridge on 7 April Smyth's brigade led the advance. As they neared Farmville they came under artillery and sharpshooter fire, and the column halted. Rain was now falling, and Smyth decided to assess the situation up-ahead with his staff. At around 11 a.m. he reached the skirmish line, where an irregular rattle of musketry was being kept up between the opposing forces. Seeing the approaching officer, a Confederate sharpshooter took careful aim at the mounted man and fired. The bullet struck home. Brigadier-General Smyth suddenly slumped to the right side of his horse, alerting his staff to the fact that he had been struck. He was quickly removed to a nearby farmhouse where the Corps hospital was located. The bullet had entered the left side of Smyth's face, where it removed a tooth on its

The High Bridge near Farmville, Virginia. Brigadier-General Thomas Alfred Smyth led his men over this bridge before he received his mortal wound. (Library of Congress)

passage towards his neck. The ball drove a fragment of cervical vertebra through his spinal cord, paralysing him.[115]

Despite the severity of his wound Smyth remained lucid, and was able to have a conversation with his surgeon about his prospects. When informed that his chances for survival were slim, the Irishman remained resolute. He told the surgeon that if one man in a hundred recovered from such an injury, he would be that man. He added 'now, Doctor, you know I am no coward, and that I am not afraid to die.' On 8 April it was decided to remove Smyth by ambulance to Burkesville Station, a distance of some 12 miles. When they were 10 miles into the journey the General began to visibly fail. Turning to his companions, Smyth told them that it was all over for him and there was no use in going any further. He was carried into the nearby house of a Colonel Burke, where he thanked the occupants for their hospitality and kindness. At 4 a.m. on the morning of 9 April 1865 Brigadier-General Thomas Alfred Smyth died. Less than twelve hours later Robert E. Lee surrendered the Army of Northern Virginia to Ulysses S. Grant at Appomattox Court House. Smyth's remains were embalmed and transported back to Wilmington, Delaware where they arrived on 15 April. He was buried the following Monday, 17 April, at Brandywine Cemetery in the city. With his death, the carriage-maker from Ballyhooly became the last Union General to be killed in the American Civil War.[116]

An Irishman in Andersonville

As many as 750,000 soldiers and 50,000 civilians died in the American Civil War. The majority were taken by sickness or violence, or a combination of the two. Even amid all this death, certain locations became notorious for the speed and efficiency with which they took lives. Some were hotly contested areas on the battlefield, which earned epithets such as 'Bloody Lane' or 'Bloody Angle'. Others were far from the front, where thousands of prisoners of war, crammed together in inadequate accommodation, fought a daily battle against hunger and disease. The most infamous and deadly of all these locations was Andersonville, in south-west Georgia.

Camp Sumter, as Andersonville was officially known, received its first Union prisoners in February 1864. It operated for fifteen months until the war's conclusion in April 1865. Originally built to hold 10,000 prisoners, it consisted of no more than sixteen acres enclosed by a stockade. By August 1864 it had been extended to twenty-six acres, as the prison population grew to 33,000 – 34 sq ft per man. With no shelter, little food and appalling sanitation, Andersonville came as near as possible to imposing a death sentence on all those sent there. During the hot Georgia summer of 1864 as many as a hundred men a day were dying. By the time it closed, of the 45,000 men who passed through Andersonville's gates, a staggering 13,000 died.[117]

One of the many Irishmen who experienced the horrors of Andersonville was Michael Dougherty. Dougherty was born on 10 May 1844 in Falcarragh, Co. Donegal, and he emigrated to the United States in 1859. At the age of eighteen he decided to enlist, mustering into the 13th Pennsylvania Cavalry on 8 August 1862 for a three-year term. It is no surprise that Dougherty chose this unit to serve in, as it had a distinct Irish character. Originally known as the 'Irish Dragoons', it was formed by James A. Gallagher of Philadelphia in September 1861. Although it had initially been intended to serve as a squadron attached to the Irish Brigade, it never served directly with that formation. Its size was increased to that of a regiment and it became the 117th Regiment (13th Cavalry), with Gallagher appointed as Colonel.[118]

Michael Dougherty was unfortunate enough to be captured not once, but twice. On 26 February 1863 he and the regiment were based in Winchester, part of Virginia's Shenandoah Valley. An alarm was raised when some supposed Confederate foragers were sighted outside the town. The Pennsylvanians set off in pursuit, capturing some of the

Rebels and driving the remainder into the camp of the 11th Virginia at Woodstock, fully twenty miles from where they had set out. With their horses exhausted the Yankees turned for home, but as they approached Fisher's Hill they were engaged by Confederates on both flanks. Within thirty minutes the 13th Pennsylvania had lost 108 men killed, wounded and captured. Among the prisoners was Dougherty, who was taken to Libby Prison in Richmond. Fortunately for Michael, at this point in the war the North and South were still routinely exchanging prisoners and he was released three months later on 26 May 1863. His first experience as a guest of the Confederacy had been mercifully brief.[119]

As 1863 continued Dougherty was quickly becoming a veteran, and he fought in his first major battle at Second Winchester that June. During the fighting he was responsible for carrying dispatches, a role he executed so well that he was presented with a gold medal for bravery by the regiment's commander Michael Kerwin, a native of County Wexford. Kerwin had taken over leadership of the 13th shortly after Second Winchester, replacing Colonel Gallagher. The horse soldiers were attached to the Army of the Potomac after the battle, joining the 2nd brigade of Brigadier-General McMurtie Gregg's 2nd division. The 12 October found the Pennsylvanians on picket duty at Jefferson, Virginia. They were positioned on the south side of the Rappahannock River, opposite Sulphur Springs.

Unknown to them, the Rebels were planning a major offensive and were about to attack the cavalrymen in force. At around 6 a.m. the Confederates streamed forward, driving in the Pennsylvanians pickets. Heavy skirmishing continued throughout the day, and the 4th Pennsylvania Cavalry were called up to help their comrades from the Keystone State. As the fighting intensified some of the Rebels decided to take up a position in an unoccupied house, a perfect position from which to fire on the Union line. Dougherty dashed from cover at the head of some of his company and sprinted across the field towards the building. The Rebels ran, and Michael and the others duly took possession of the house. For the next few hours they fought off attack after attack as they clung tenaciously to what they had won. Eventually the Confederates fed more men into the fight, and by 5 p.m. they succeeded in driving the 4th and 13th Pennsylvania back. With their backs to the river many of the Union men were cut off and could not escape to their own lines. The 13th lost a total of 163 men killed, wounded and captured. Once again Michael was captured, but this time there would be no exchange.[120]

Michael Dougherty remained a prisoner of the Rebels from 12 October 1863 to 12 April 1865. Throughout this time he kept a diary, charting his experiences in various Southern prisons such as Libby, Pemberton, Belle Isle and Andersonville. The Donegal man spent his first months as a prisoner in Pemberton, Richmond. The building was a large former tobacco warehouse, 30ft wide and 90ft deep, with three floors. In late 1863 it accommodated some 700 Union prisoners. Dougherty recorded that 'no one can form an idea of what suffering there is here, and no pen can describe the hardships we have to endure'. There were 300 prisoners on his floor, who were kept 'more like hogs than men'. The soldiers were packed so tightly that it was impossible to move around. To pass the time the half-naked men spent much of the day catching lice, with mealtime offering the only distraction. The rations they received were paltry – on 9 December it consisted of two biscuits and four ounces of pork per man. After two months as a prisoner Dougherty estimated that he had already lost 25 pounds in weight. Those who became sick were unable to lift themselves from the floor, and in the cramped conditions they risked the additional injury of being trampled by other inmates.[121]

On 20 December the Confederate Quartermaster called the prisoners together, telling the men that boxes had arrived for some of them. A month previously, on 23 November, the nineteen-year-old Donegal man had written to his mother in Bristol, Pennsylvania, asking her to send him a Christmas present with some 'shirts and notions' in it. Now

Andersonville Prison, Georgia, on 17 August 1864. Michael Dougherty writes in his diary for the day: 'No prisoners left here today or yesterday. Alfred Friend, Co. F, 12th NYC has just informed me that he is the only man alive out of fifty-three of his regiment.' (Library of Congress)

was the time Michael would find out if his mother had been successful. All the men remained silent and expectant as the names of those lucky few to receive boxes were read out. At last, Michael's name was called. He recorded in his diary: 'Oh! How glad I was when I heard that name!'[122]

Michael was still in Pemberton when Christmas Day 1863 arrived. He recorded the day in his diary:

> Christmas Day, 1863, and still in the Confederacy. Thinking of our friends at home, enjoying themselves, and condition

we are in. The most barbarous country would hardly treat a prisoner thus. One of my regiment died last night. It was a relief to a great deal of suffering. There was a hole under his arm large enough to put your fist in. Rations two biscuits, half a loaf of corn dodger and two spoonfuls of molasses, for our Christmas present, but I will attend to my box to-day. The Richmond papers state that the stench from the prison is endangering the health and the lives of all in the City, and it would be well to remove those "Lincoln hirelings" to where scant fare and cold weather would reduce them in number; consequently we will be removed to Bell Isle.[123]

Michael was transferred to Belle Isle, an island in the middle of the James River at Richmond, on 28 December 1863. He described the prison as an area of about six acres, enclosed by an earthwork and ditch. The prisoners occupied a low-lying and exposed 'barren waste' with no tree cover and only a small number of tents. He summed it up on 29 December: 'This is a horrible place. Pemberton we thought was bad, but nothing compared to Bell Isle.'[124]

Unfortunately for the Irishman his prison experiences were growing continually worse, as he moved from one hell-hole to the next. On 8 February 1864 he boarded a train in Richmond with 600 other prisoners. Some of the men thought they were going to be exchanged, but their hopes were dashed when the locomotive headed south. The men arrived at Camp Sumter, Andersonville, on 15 February. The prison was still new, but would soon become vastly overcrowded. Michael tried to occupy his time by visiting different parts of the camp and recording any events of note in his diary. It is a stark record of the human misery he and others experienced during his time in the exposed compound. Unsurprisingly, his diary is dominated by new prisoners, the death of comrades, and rations.[125]

18 April 1864: About five hundred more prisoners came in to-day from Cahaba, Alabama. Bernard Tolen, Co. D, died to-day.[126]

15 May 1864: We can see wagons haul away bodies from the dead-house, like so much dirt; as many as twenty bodies piled on one wagon. Upwards of fifteen hundred men have died since we came here.[127]

21 May 1864: Prisoners dying of dropsy; when they are dead, their bodies swell up as large as barrels. There is quite a fight over a dead man's pants; when a prisoner dies, his shoes, stockings, shirt, pants and cap are stripped from him. One prisoner will almost kill another to gain possession of them.[128]

20 July 1864: One hundred and thirty prisoners died yesterday; it is so hot we are almost roasted. There were 127 of my regiment captured the day I was, and of that number eighty-one have since died, and the rest are more dead than alive; exposure and long confinement is doing its work among us.[129]

There was an interesting visitor to the prison on 13 November 1864:

All the Irish who could walk were called to the gate this afternoon by a Col. McNeill of the 10th Tennessee (Rebel) regiment, to see if any of them would take the oath to join the rebel service. Not an Irishman enlisted, but two Yankees did, one from Connecticut and the other from a New York regiment; so you see the Irish are the most loyal.

The following day Dougherty added:

> Webb called on me to-day; we had a talk over the
> excitement caused by the appeal to the Irish; he says
> McNeill is no true Irishman or he would not try to degrade
> Ireland and her people by making such a proposition.

The 10th Tennessee had been formed of Irishmen from Nashville in 1861, and 'Col. McNeill' was in fact Colonel John G. O'Neill. The remnants of the unit surrendered with the Army of Tennessee in 1865 following its defeat at the Battle of Bentonville, North Carolina.[130]

Somehow during those desperate months Michael managed to stay alive. However, December 1864 found him seriously ill and in the camp hospital. He scribbled in his diary on the 10th:

> My diary is full; it is too bad, but cannot get any more
> [paper]. Good bye all; I did not think it would hold out
> so long when I commenced. Yours sufferingly, Michael
> Dougherty, Co. B, 13th Pa. Volunteer Cavalry.

However, Michael pulled through and made it to the end of the war. Incredibly, his tribulations were not over. On 23 April 1865 he boarded a ship at Vicksburg, Mississippi, that was intended to take him and many other prisoners home. Her name was the *Sultana*, and she set off up the Mississippi with between 2,200 and 2,400 Union soldiers aboard, many of whom were Andersonville survivors. Their destination was St Louis, Missouri; by the 26 April they had travelled as far as Memphis, Tennessee. In the early hours of 27 April one of the *Sultana*'s boilers exploded, enveloping the boat in flames. Some 1,800 passengers lost their lives, in what remains the worst maritime disaster in United States history. Michael was one of the few survivors – he had once again beaten the odds.[131]

Michael Dougherty of the 13th Pennsylvania Cavalry in later life. (*Prison Diary of Michael Dougherty*)

Michael Dougherty returned to Bristol, Pennsylvania, and his mother and sisters on 27 June 1865. He went on to marry Rose Magee, with whom he had twelve children. In the post-war years he worked in the US Mint in Philadelphia and served as a Bristol Council Member between 1880 and 1882. He was also an active member of the Ancient Order of Hibernians.

The actions that led to his capture on 12 October 1863 were recognised later in life. On 23 January 1897 he was awarded the Congressional Medal of Honor for his part in the battle. His citation read:

> At the head of a detachment of his company dashed across
> an open field, exposed to a deadly fire from the enemy, and
> succeeded in dislodging them from an unoccupied house,
> which he and his comrades defended for several hours
> against repeated attacks, thus preventing the enemy from
> flanking the position of the Union forces.

The Falcarragh native published his prison diary in 1908, providing an invaluable insight into the terrible conditions experienced by Union troops in Andersonville. Having survived so many trials in early life, Michael Dougherty went on to live well into his eighties. He died on 19 February 1930, and is buried in St Mark's Roman Catholic churchyard in Bristol, Pennsylvania.[132]

THREE

The Wider War

The American Civil War was experienced to one degree or another by far more than the 170,000 or so Irishmen who donned Union blue or Confederate grey. Many in the Irish-American communities of the North found fewer and fewer reasons to support the continuation of the struggle as the war progressed. Although the majority of those Irish at the front remained committed to the fight, many at home had lost faith, in the face of rising casualties and the perceived changing focus of the war. The decision to institute a draft to compel enlistment in the army led to an explosion of violence in New York in July 1863. The rioters were largely Irish, and they targeted symbols of the Republican administration, the black community, and even their fellow countrymen in uniform who were perceived as supporting the government.

It was also in 1863 that a war of subterfuge came to the shores of Ireland, as the Confederate States attempted to use agents to stem the flow of Irish emigration to the North, and ultimately into Union armies and navies. Allegations of illegal recruitment by the Union in Ireland were rife, and the one case where it certainly happened ended in a man from Queenstown (Cobh) playing a role in the Civil War that would have been unimaginable for him only a few months previously.

Not all the Irishmen at the front were engaged in the fighting. Some were there to record these dramatic events as they unfolded, and to create a record of what warfare in the 1860s was like. Two of the most notable were an artist and a photographer who accompanied Union armies in both victory and defeat in an effort to inform those at home about what was taking place. Irish women were also an ever-present with the armies, and wives and sisters both North and South sought to provide stability, care and comfort for those engaged in the fighting. A small number of women went a step further, and took up a gun to march side-by-side with the men in the ranks.

Killed by his own

Although the root causes of the American Civil War lay with slavery, few of the Irish who fought for the Union did so to free the slaves. David Power Conyngham, who had briefly served with the Irish Brigade and wrote that unit's history in 1867, explained why many of the Irish had enlisted in 1861:

> The Irish felt that not only was the safety of the great
> Republic, the home of their exiled race, at stake, but also,
> that the great principles of democracy were at issue with
> the aristocratic doctrines of monarchism. Should the latter
> prevail, there was no longer any hope for the struggling
> nationalists of the Old World. The Irish soldier did not ask
> whether the colored race were better off as bondsmen or

freedmen; he was not going to fight for an abstract idea. He felt that the safety and welfare of his adopted country and its glorious Constitution were imperilled; he, therefore, willingly threw himself into the breach to sustain the flag that sheltered him when persecuted and exiled from his own country, the laws that protected him, and the country that, like a loving mother, poured forth the richness of her bosom to sustain him.[133]

As the war dragged on and casualties mounted, many in the Irish communities of the North began to question the direction of the conflict. Opposition to the war began to solidify in late 1862. Severe Irish losses on the battlefields of Antietam and Fredericksburg led some to wonder if native-born prejudices were causing Irish soldiers to be used as cannon fodder. Worse still was Abraham Lincoln's announcement of the Emancipation Proclamation in September 1862. Emancipation for the slaves could mean a flood of competition in the unskilled labour market that was vital for the survival of the Irish urban poor. The Irish by and large occupied a position on the lowest rung of the ladder of white Northern society. Although they had been the subject of significant discrimination, they had always been one step above enslaved blacks – emancipation could change that.[134]

A major problem for the Union war effort in 1863 was the fall off in the number of men volunteering for the military. By this time few were under any illusions about either the duration of the war or its cost in human lives. On 3 March 1863 Congress passed the Conscription Act, designed to bolster numbers in Union forces. Each state would be set a quota for enlistment, and numbers would be supplemented by a draft if they failed to secure the requisite number of volunteers. Federal provost marshals were empowered to arrest draft evaders or resisters. Those who had little desire to die at the front and who did not agree with the Union's war aims could now be coerced into fighting. As the draft applied to citizens only, it was whites alone who were subject to it. In addition anyone who could pay $300 was exempted. The white poor in cities like New York were incensed. In their view the wealthy could buy their way out of service, sending the poor off to die in order to emancipate blacks, who could then flood northwards and take their jobs. The fact that free blacks in New York would not be subject to the draft was also a cause of friction. The situation was a powder keg, waiting for a match.[135]

Monday 13 July 1863 was the date set for the first draft in New York. The labourers of the city had decided to protest the draft en-mass,

The draft wheel being turned before men's names were picked out as part of the selection process. It was the imminent implementation of this draft that led to the riots in New York in July 1863. (Library of Congress)

and instead of reporting for work took to the streets to show their displeasure. The protest broke down into a riot, which swept through the city for five days. A vast amount of property was destroyed by the rioters, as homes and premises were attacked, looted and burned. The rioters also vented their anger at the local black community, murdering a number of them in horrendous circumstances and even burning down the Colored Orphan Asylum. The majority of those involved came from the city's poorer areas, and included large numbers of the Irish community.

The military were called in to try to assist the police and quell the disturbances. Just as a large number of the rioters were Irish, so were many of those who were tasked with restoring order. One of the victims was Robert Nugent from Co. Down, Colonel of the 69th New York and later commander of the Irish Brigade. In July 1863 he was the Acting Assistant Provost Marshal for Southern New York, with a mandate to enforce the draft. As a result of his position rioters targeted his home, which they broke into, looting and destroying its contents.[136]

Another who found himself in the wrong place at the wrong time was Colonel Henry F. O'Brien. He had been born in Ireland around 1823, but little else is known about his life prior to the American Civil War. He served as a captain of Company H in the 155th New York Infantry, part of Corcoran's Irish Legion, from 12 October 1862 until his honourable discharge from that regiment on 6 February 1863. In June, O'Brien was given permission to recruit soldiers in order to re-constitute the 11th New York Infantry. The original 11th had been known as the Ellsworth Zouaves, and had mustered out of service in 1862. Permission to re-establish the unit had initially been granted to James C. Burke in May of 1863, but this authorisation was revoked and passed to O'Brien instead. Colonel O'Brien was busily recruiting men for his regiment in New York when the draft riots erupted.[137]

Henry O'Brien quickly offered his services and those of the men he had recruited to the police. Reports as to the sequence of events that followed are somewhat confused. What is known is that on the morning of Tuesday 14 July a large mob had assembled at the junction of Second Avenue and Thirty-Fourth Street. According to the *New York Times*, the crowd became incensed when they learned that O'Brien and his men were going to march on them. The rioters proceeded to O'Brien's nearby home, and forced his family onto the street while they looted the premises. Some 300 New York police arrived to confront the rioters,

Among the targets of the Draft Rioters were New York's colored community. One of the most infamous acts of the week was the burning of the Colored Orphan Asylum. (Library of Congress)

and they marched down Second Avenue through a hail of missiles in an attempt to clear the area. This was the fateful moment when Colonel O'Brien arrived on the scene at the head of his men.[138]

The colonel had brought two companies of the 11th New York and two artillery pieces under the command of Lieutenant Eagleson. He joined forces with the police, and moved his men forward to confront the Second Avenue crowd. There are a number of versions as to what transpired next. One witness recalled that:

> He [O'Brien] unlimbered his pieces, notified the mob in the streets to disperse, and after waiting for them to do so a sufficient time, fired; he had elevated his guns so as to shoot over the heads of the crowd, giving as his reason that he did not want to hurt them if scaring would do as well.

According to some other accounts, far from trying to avoid civilian injury, O'Brien had ridden up to the crowd and fired his pistol into them. Whether through some errant firing by his soldiers, a mishap with artillery blanks, or indiscriminate shooting by the colonel himself, the end-result was that a woman and child fell dead in front of the 11th New York's position. Regardless of what actually happened, the crowd had no doubts about who was responsible. They retreated, but did not go far. The mob now had one focus: dozens of eyes stared at Colonel Henry O'Brien, and they bore an unquenchable thirst for revenge.[139]

It was now around 2 p.m. in the afternoon. As the situation had appeared to die down, the Colonel made the bizarre decision to stray from the safety of his men. The *New York Tribune* related that he went into a nearby drug store in search of refreshments. When he re-emerged onto the street he found that the mob had reformed, silently surrounding him. Drawing his sword and revolver, he walked out into the crowd, presumably in the hope of regaining the safety of his men.

Suddenly, a man emerged from behind O'Brien and struck him across the back of the head. Staggering, the Irishman was quickly overwhelmed and disappeared beneath a wave of assailants who rained blows down on him. Despite the violence of the attack, and unfortunately for Henry O'Brien, his end would not be a quick one.[140]

The rioters were bent on vengeance. Having secured control of the street from the authorities they were free to deal with O'Brien at their leisure. After his initial beating he was dragged to a nearby lamp-post, where he was strung up by a rope. Now covered in blood and breathing heavily, he was cut down and hurled back into the street, where he lay for an hour being periodically kicked and pelted with stones. He was being dragged around the street when a correspondent from *Harper's Weekly* happened on the scene:

> As I arrived at the corner of Thirty-fourth Street and Second Avenue, the rioters were dragging the body of a man along the sidewalk with a rope. It was difficult to obtain any information from the bystanders who were terror struck by the savage fury of the mob. I ascertained, however, that the body was that of Colonel O'Brien of the Eleventh New York. There was not a policeman or soldier within view of whom inquiry could be made. 'What did they kill him for?' I asked a man leaning against a lamp-post. 'Bedad, I suppose it was to square accounts,' replied he. 'There was a woman and child kilt there below a while ago by the sojers, and in coarse a sojer had to suffer.' The brutal roughs who surrounded the body fired pistols at it occasionally, and pelted it with brick-bats and paving stones.[141]

Incredibly, Henry O'Brien was not yet dead. Another witness described his condition: 'The head was nearly one mass of gore, while the clothes were also saturated with the crimson fluid of life.' Occasionally the 'extended mass of flesh' that had once been Colonel O'Brien would raise his head, only to be struck once again by those surrounding him. Some accounts suggest that he clung to life for up to six hours in this way, all the time being periodically beaten. Eventually his horrendous suffering ended, and the Colonel died on the street only a short distance from his home. Shortly afterwards the riot moved on, making it possible for his body to be recovered and taken to Bellevue Hospital.

Following the murder a substantial reward was offered for the apprehension of those involved. A number of men including Patrick Keegan, Patrick O'Brien and later Thomas Kealy were arrested. All were Irish. The suffering of 14 July marked only the beginning for Henry O'Brien's widow, Anna. On 30 January 1864 the *New York Herald* published a heart-rending letter she had felt compelled to write:[142]

> I am the widow of Colonel Henry F. O'Brien, who lost his life while endeavoring to protect this, the proud city of his adoption, from the ravages of a plundering mob during the riots of July last. Slaughtered with a barbarity seldom equalled by savages, his poor mangled remains were unceremoniously hurried off to a pauper's grave, where they still lie unnoticed and forgotten. I was myself forced to fly from the fury of the mob, who ransacked my house and destroyed or stole everything I possessed. Thus, at one fell swoop, were carried away home, husband and all that rendered life comfortable and happy.[143]

The distraught widow found that all her appeals for the honourable reburial of her husband had fallen on deaf ears, as had her request for a pension to support herself. Her letter was a desperate attempt to have someone in officialdom take notice. Whatever the outcome of her appeals for a pension, Anna O'Brien did not have her wish for a suitable memorial for her husband fulfilled. Henry O'Brien today lies in an unmarked grave in Section 1 West, Avenue E, Plot 10 of Calvary Cemetery on Long Island. It remains unclear if Colonel O'Brien was the heartless villain the mob believed him to be, who fired indiscriminately at a woman and her child, or if he was simply in the wrong place at the wrong time, a man trying to do his best in difficult circumstances. His death, falling at the hands of enraged fellow Irishmen at the junction of Second Avenue and Thirty-Fourth Street on that July day was certainly not the one he might have imagined for himself the previous June, as he set about organising his regiment.[144]

The New York Draft Riots were over by 17 July. The worst riots in American history, they had left at least 105 people dead. Although the rioters were not exclusively Irish, it has been estimated that at least two-thirds were from the New York Irish community. This is perhaps not surprising given that one in four of the city's nearly 800,000-strong population in 1860 were Irish-born, and the vast majority of Irish dwelt among New York's poor. Many Irish-American soldiers at the front could not understand the rioter's actions. Peter Welsh, who was serving with the 28th Massachusetts Infantry, Irish Brigade wrote to his wife on 17 July:[145]

> I am sorry to hear that there is such disgracefull riots in New York. I hope it will not get near to you nor anoy you. I read a full account of it in yesterdays paper. The report was up to twelve oclock wensday night. I see they tried the virtue of grape and canister on them and it had a very good effect. The originaters of those riots should be hung like dogs. They are agents of jef davis and had their plans laid [to] start those riots simutanesly with Lees raid into Pensilvenia. I hope the authorutys will use canister freely. It will bring the bloody cutthroats to their censes.[146]

The failure of the government to tackle the neglect and prejudices that faced many of the urban poor had contributed greatly to the riots. Unfortunately for the Irish, the perception that they had been central to the disturbances seriously damaged their reputation in the North. Despite the efforts of ethnic units such as the Irish Brigade and Corcoran's Irish Legion on the battlefields of the war, and the general manpower contribution made by the Irish community, it was a view that would persist. As Susannah Ural has noted, it contributed 'to an image that would endure for decades of the Irish as disloyal, violent, and threatening to all that was good in America.'[147]

Confederates in Ireland

As the American Civil War progressed, the Confederacy grew increasingly concerned about rumours that the Union were recruiting directly in Ireland. With the conflict dragging on and the need for manpower increasing, Ireland was an obvious location from where to source additional soldiers. The North fervently denied that they were engaged in any such activities, but both the Confederacy and the British government had their doubts. Whatever the reality or otherwise of official US approval, there is little doubt that there were those in Ireland who sought to profit from inducing their fellow countrymen to emigrate and enlist in return for financial reward.

That the British were concerned about potential recruitment can be seen in a letter written on 16 April 1863 by British Foreign Secretary Earl Russell to Charles Francis Adams, Lincoln's ambassador to Britain. Russell claimed that within the last fortnight 1,278 emigrants, influenced by a bounty of $250 or $300, had sailed to the United States with the intention of joining the Union Army. He added that there were upwards of 800 youths waiting to sail from Queenstown (now Cobh) with the same aim. Adams replied that neither he nor any of the other

US consuls had anything to do with it, and that no American citizens had been given authority to recruit British subjects. In the absence of any material evidence to suggest otherwise, there was little the British could do.[148]

Confederates in Europe gradually became convinced that the stories of Federal recruitment in Ireland were true. On 8 June 1863 James Murray Mason, the Confederate representative in Britain, wrote to Robert Dowling, the Rebel's commercial agent in Cork. Mason wanted Dowling to find out as much as he could about the alleged recruitment:

> ... these enlistments are made by the Federal agencies under false pretences, such, it is said, as pretended engagements for laborers on railroads in the United States or as farm hands. You will best know in what manner most successfully to conduct these inquires, with a view to get at the facts, however they may be disguised.

In order to assist Dowling, the Confederate Government decided to send 'two or three Irishmen, long residents of our country, to act as far as they can in arresting these unlawful acts of the enemy by communicating directly with the people.'[149]

The first agent selected was Lieutenant James L. Capston of Company D, 10th Virginia Cavalry. The Confederate Secretary of State, Judah P. Benjamin informed him in a letter of 3 July 1863 that he was to travel to Ireland and use legitimate means to counteract the work of agents of the United States believed to be operating there:

> The duty which is proposed to entrust to you is that of a private and confidential agent of this government, for the purpose of proceeding to Ireland, and there using all legitimate means to enlighten the population as to the

true nature and character of the contest now waged in this continent, with the view of defeating the attempts made by the agents of the United States to obtain in Ireland recruits for their armies. It is understood that under the guise of assisting needy persons to emigrate, a regular organisation has been formed of agents in Ireland who leave untried no method of deceiving the laboring population into emigrating for the ostensible purpose of seeking employment in the United States, but really for recruiting the Federal armies.[150]

Benjamin stressed that Capston was to keep secret that he was in the employ of the Confederate government, and only use legitimate means to achieve his goals. Under no circumstances was he to break any British laws. Capston was instructed to make contacts in the press and with persons of influence in order to get his message across. He told him to:

Inform them [the Irish] by every means you can devise, of the true purpose of those who seek to induce them to emigrate. Explain to them the nature of the warfare which is carried on here. Picture to them the fate of their unhappy countrymen who have already fallen victims to the arts of the Federals. Relate to them the story of Meagher's Brigade, its formation and its fate. Explain to them that they will be called on to meet Irishmen in battle, and thus to imbrue their hands in the blood of their own friends, and perhaps kinsmen, in a quarrel which does not concern them, and in which all the feelings of a common humanity should induce them to refuse taking part against us.

For his services in Ireland Lieutenant Capston was to be paid £21 a month, and if he required any additional funds for activities such as printing he could obtain them from his handler in England.[151]

Lieutenant Capston arrived in London on 5 September 1863, where he met with Special Agent Henry Hotze. Capston was to report back to the Confederacy through Hotze. He set off for Ireland straight away, travelling first to Dublin and then proceeding to Limerick, Galway and Cork. The lieutenant published a number of letters in the papers and met with the clergy to spread his message. Among the propaganda he produced was a poster decrying the supposed actions of Massachusetts soldiers against Catholics in the South. In large type it read: 'Overthrown! The Blessed Host Scattered On The Ground! Benediction Veil Made a Horse Cover of! All The Sacred Vessels Carried Off! The Priest Imprisoned and Afterwards Exposed on an Island to Alligators and Snakes!' Lieutenant Capston stayed in Ireland until May 1864, after which it seems he returned to the Confederacy.[152]

At least two other Confederate agents were dispatched to Ireland. One, Captain Lalor, sailed from Wilmington, North Carolina, sometime after 29 February 1864, and reported to Hotze in London in April. Unfortunately no other records relating to his mission survive. The other agent was Father John Bannon. Born in Roosky, Co. Roscommon in 1829, Father Bannon had been ordained in 1853 and moved to the Diocese of St Louis, Missouri. When war broke out he became the Chaplain of the 1st Missouri Confederate Brigade. He served with them throughout the Western Theater until they were captured following the fall of Vicksburg, Mississippi in July 1863. The loss of his brigade presented the Confederate government with an opportunity to use Father Bannon elsewhere, and he was duly contacted by Judah P. Benjamin. On 4 September 1863 he wrote to Bannon copying the same instructions he had issued to Lieutenant Capston. Father Bannon's position as a member of the Catholic clergy also allowed Benjamin to expand on the priest's mission:

> If, in order to fully carry out the objects of the Government as above expressed, you should deem it advisable to go to Rome for the purpose of obtaining such sanction from the sovereign pontiff as will strengthen your hands and give efficiency to your action, you are at liberty to do so, as well as to invite to your assistance any Catholic prelate from the Northern States known to you to share your convictions of the justice of our cause and of the duty of laboring for its success.[153]

Father Bannon was to be paid £20 a month for his work, and as with Capston he was provided with a letter of introduction to Henry Hotze. He was additionally entrusted with the sum of $1,212.50 in gold to cover his travel expenses and salary. By the 31 October 1863 Father Bannon was staying at the Angel Hotel in Dublin, and had set about his mission with zeal. He quickly made contact with the press, assisting in preparing pro-Southern articles in the *Nation*. He created the *nom de plume* 'Sacerdos' (Latin for priest) to use for the circulars and letters he produced. He also took on speaking engagements around the country to spread his message. The priest produced 2,000 pro-Southern handbills which he dispatched to Queenstown and Galway to be handed out to potential emigrants and posted in boarding houses that they used prior to departure. In early 1864 he had 3,000 copies of a broadside sent to parish priests, the text of which implied the Pope's support for the South and decried the Yankees as the descendants of Cromwell.

Bannon's tireless work did not go unnoticed in Richmond. On 22 April 1864, Benjamin wrote to Hotze telling him that he was 'much gratified with the zeal, discretion and ability displayed by the Revd Mr Bannon in the service undertaken by him, and desire you should continue to provide him with the necessary means for continuing his labours as long as he remains satisfied that his efforts are useful to our cause.' Jefferson Davis was also pleased with the reports coming from Ireland.

Father John Bannon, Chaplain of the 1st Missouri Confederate Brigade and later a Rebel agent in Ireland. (Irish Jesuit Archives)

The President of the Confederacy annotated one of Father Bannon's reports with: 'Course of the agent is very satisfactory.' On 28 May 1864 the Roscommon priest decided that his mission was accomplished and that he had done as much as possible. He did not return to the South, but stayed in Ireland where he became a Jesuit. He died on 14 July 1913 at the age of eighty-four, and is buried in the Jesuit Plot at Glasnevin Cemetery, Dublin.[154]

Confederate agents like Lieutenant Capston and Father Bannon were not the only men who travelled to Ireland from the South to try to stem the flow of emigrants. Robert Atkins was the son of the local Episcopal clergyman in Mallow, Revd Mr Atkins. Robert had long been something of a military adventurer. He had served as an officer in the Royal Cork City Artillery in the 1850s, before heading to Italy to fight with Garibaldi in 1860 as part of the 'British Legion'. While in Italy he struck up a friendship with an American called Chatham Roberdeau Wheat, a Southerner who had been born in Virginia but grew up in Louisiana. This encounter brought Robert to America on the eve of the Civil War.[155]

In New Orleans Wheat organised the 1st Louisiana Special Battalion, a motley group of natives and immigrants (including many Irish) who would prove extraordinarily ill-disciplined but courageous in a fight. They soon took on the moniker of the 'Louisiana Tigers'. Robert Atkins became a captain in the outfit, and served with them in the first major battle of the war at Bull Run. One colourful account of the Irishman's service claimed that: 'It was Captain Atkins who led Wheat's Battalion at Manassas, after the noble Wheat fell wounded, leading the celebrated charge of the Louisiana Tigers with a bare shillalah.'[156]

After his service with the Tigers, Atkins went on to become aide-de-camp on the staff of Major-General Arnold Elzey, who commanded the Department of Richmond. It was while in this position that personal family business necessitated his return to Ireland. Finding himself back in his Mallow home in early 1864, Atkins decided to try to help the

Southern cause from afar by writing to the Bishop of Kerry regarding Irish emigration and enlistment in Union armies. Dated 9 January 1864, the letter touches on many themes that would have been familiar to both Capston and Bannon:

> Is it not sad, my Lord, to witness the flower of our peasantry, at this moment in America, imbruing their hands in each others blood? – Why does the Irishman, who craves for liberty at home, and who complains of mis-government here, support, at the risk of his life, the most degraded despotism the world has yet seen? And why does he … enrol himself under the 'abolition banners' of Abraham Lincoln, and congratulate himself that he is on a crusade, to grant an unsolicited freedom to three millions of 'Africans', who are better clothed, better lodged, and beyond all better fed then he is himself?

Atkins than proceeded to inform the bishop what he felt it was that led the Irish to fight for the North:

> His own adventurous spirit – the distressed condition of his native land, and then by far the greatest inducement – the enormous bounty paid by the Yankee Government for fighting material. What spirited young fellow, who perhaps never made a note in his life, can stand the golden bait of seven hundred and seventy-seven dollars.[157]

His family business forced Robert Atkins's resignation from the Confederate Army in February 1864. The Bishop of Kerry's reaction to his letter is unrecorded, but Atkins views did persuade at least one person as to the validity of the South's cause. His younger brother John headed across the Atlantic in February 1864, taking up arms with John

Singleton Mosby, the famed 'Gray Ghost' who led Rebel Partisan cavalry. John's Southern adventure did not last long. The Richmond Examiner revealed his fate:

> In a charge upon the enemy made by Mosby's band at Upperville on the 29 October, fell mortally wounded JOHN ATKINS, a private trooper, the son of the Rev. Mr. Atkins, an eminent Espiscopal Clergyman of Mallow, in the County of Cork, Ireland ... who arrived in the Confederacy in the month of March last, with the purpose of throwing himself into our struggle for independence, and at once purchased a horse and joined Mosby, under whose command he has participated in all the dashing exploits of that noble partisan leader. Thus has fallen another of the gallant young soldiers whom European countries have contributed to our devoted armies.[158]

John's older brother Robert never lost his love for the South. In early 1870 he returned to America to participate in a hunting trip to Arkansas, from which he never returned. He died while on the holiday, at the age of thirty-nine.[159]

Just how real was direct Union recruitment in Ireland? There is no evidence that the United States ever sanctioned official recruitment in the country, but there are incidents where men were fooled by unscrupulous emigration agents, who were seeking a pay-off in the shape of the Union bounty given to volunteers. An example was the plight of 120 Irish labourers who arrived in Portland, Maine, on 11 March 1864 expecting to begin work on the railroads. They were taken to Boston where they were locked in a warehouse and plied with whiskey. An official recruiter arrived two days later, with police blocking the exits to prevent escape. The local Irish community was outraged, and stormed the warehouse, breaking through the police cordon and freeing those inside. However, they came too late for seven of the Irishmen, who had already been shipped off to join the 20th Maine Infantry. While all this had been going on the agent who arranged the ruse in Ireland, a Mr Finney, was arrested for illegal recruitment.[160]

The Confederate agents sent to Ireland seem to have had a negligible impact on emigration to the United States. Despite their best efforts, the potential of a better life across the Atlantic remained a huge draw for many in Ireland. What is beyond doubt is the importance that the Confederate government placed in their mission, as they sought any means possible to stem the flow of Irishmen into the ranks of the Yankee Army. The decision to send agents directly to Ireland brought a war of subterfuge to the country, as Rebels and Yankees alike vied in print and prose for the hearts and minds of the Irish populace.[161]

The Queenstown Affair

On the morning of 3 November 1863, the Federal sloop of war USS *Kearsarge* steamed into Queenstown harbour, County Cork. Anchoring to the east of the Spit Light, members of her crew crowded the deck to get a look at the town. While they waited to hear if any of them would be lucky enough to be granted a brief shore pass, some of the *Kearsarge* officers prepared for quite a different mission. Their activities would cause a major diplomatic incident between the United States and Great Britain, which would become known as the 'Queenstown Affair'. Meanwhile, for one local in the town, the arrival of the *Kearsarge* was destined to dramatically alter his life.[162]

The *Kearsarge* was in European waters on the hunt for Confederate raiders who had been attacking US shipping. As the warship dropped anchor a fleet of small boats filled with locals rowed out to meet it; some had produce to sell, while others were just eager to get a good look at the Union vessel. Coal Heaver Charles Poole of the *Kearsarge* thought Queenstown a small town considering how busy the port was, and he remarked that the old houses on the shore gave the settlement an 'antique' look. For some among the crew it was a familiar sight. Quarter Gunner John Dempsey knew it well, and even encountered people who knew his family among those who had journeyed out to greet them. As Queenstown was a neutral port, the local Examining Officer sought out the captain of the *Kearsarge*, John A. Winslow, to inform him that the vessel could stay for no longer than twenty-four hours. However, Winslow had already set off for Cork to visit the US Consul Edwin Eastman. His deputy, Lieutenant Commander James Thornton, informed the official that he would leave the port when his captain ordered him to, and not before. The local media quickly condemned the warship's actions as defiance of the law. Things had got off to a bad start.[163]

One of the crew who was granted shore leave was captain of the forecastle Jimmy Haley. He was from nearby Ringaskiddy, and was allowed to go home to visit his sister. Jimmy had been a seaman all his life, and it had been about twenty years since he had left Cork. He had previously served aboard the British *Shamrock*, before signing on in the US service. While in Ringaskiddy, Haley suggested to a number of the locals that there may be positions available aboard the *Kearsarge*. It was common practice for both Union and Confederate vessels to fill up their compliment of crew when in port, regardless of nationality. However, to suggest it in Ireland was a risky business, as any enlistment would breach the Foreign Enlistments Act, which made it illegal to recruit or enlist for foreign service in British territory. It is not clear if Haley was acting under orders from his superiors by spreading this news, but it seems probable that he was. Regardless, word passed like wildfire around Ringaskiddy and Queenstown that the American ship was recruiting.[164]

A large number of men soon made their way out to the *Kearsarge* to see if the rumours were true. Ringaskiddy man John Dunn had a boat, and he was asked by a number of locals to take them to the ship. On Wednesday 4 November he brought John Sullivan, Edward Pyburne, Thomas Murphy and George Patterson out, and the following day provided the same service for Denis Leary. All were Ringaskiddy men, and Dunn later stated that they were so poor that none of them were able to pay him for the journey. A large number of Queenstown men also went out to the vessel.

Patrick Kennedy went onto the *Kearsarge* at 2 p.m. on 3 November with Thomas Verling and two others. He was told that he would be signed on as a Landsman, the lowest rank in the US Navy, and be paid $12 a month. Patrick was taken to be examined by the ship's doctor where he was asked to strip and was medically assessed. Edward Lynch from Queenstown boarded the *Kearsarge* with Daniel O'Connell of Whitepoint and John Connelly of Bishop's Street. The three men were treated to their dinner and supper aboard, and were also inspected by the doctor. Unfortunately for Lynch, he was deemed too short and failed the examination. Both O'Connell and Connelly passed, and briefly returned to shore to say their goodbyes. Daniel O'Connell probably went to visit his mother, Mrs Buckley, at her house by the town's chapel to give her the news of his imminent departure.[165]

Captain Winslow returned from Cork on 5 November, and the sloop made ready for sea. Departing that afternoon the new men quickly found themselves subjected to the full rigours of life before the mast, as heavy seas caused most of them to become violently seasick. Back in Queenstown another storm was brewing. The officers of the *Kearsarge* had been less than discreet regarding the recruitment, and it came to the attention of a Confederate agent then in the town, most probably Lieutenant James Capston. Hardly believing his luck, Capston alerted the British authorities, sparking a major diplomatic incident. Correspondence flew between the British Foreign Secretary Earl Russell and US Ambassador to Britain Charles Francis Adams. The British

The USS *Kearsarge*, which illegally recruited men while anchored at Queenstown in 1863, and carried Michael Ahern from unemployment to become a recipient of the Medal of Honor. (Library of Congress)

Government were incensed at this seemingly flagrant abuse of their sovereignty, and the Lincoln administration grew concerned about the potential damage it may cause to the already fragile relationship between the two countries. The US Secretary of the Navy investigated the incident, and matters grew so serious that Lincoln himself became involved, declaring that 'we should remove, so far as is possible, every plausible ground of complaint of violation of British neutrality laws by our agents.'[166]

The major problem for the Federal case was that John Dunn, Patrick Kennedy and Edward Lynch had come forward with information that suggested the *Kearsarge* had been openly recruiting. Kennedy also claimed in his declaration to have seen US Consul Edwin Eastman aboard the vessel as he waited to be examined by the ship's doctor. This made matters even worse, as it implied official sanction had been given for the actions of the *Kearsarge*. The fact that Dunn and Lynch were available to give statements is not surprising, as Dunn simply carried men out to the boat, while Lynch had been rejected by the ship's doctor as a result of his short stature. The fact that Patrick Kennedy chose not to sail is harder to explain, as he appears to have passed the medical exam. It is also strange that he was able to identify the US Consul aboard, a man he had no reason to know. It is possible that Lieutenant Capston, having learned about the *Kearsarge*'s activities, decided to 'plant' perspective recruits aboard to add to the case he was building against the Union vessel.[167]

Meanwhile, out at sea, Captain Winslow was going through the process of adding the new men to his crew. He was keen not to flagrantly violate British law by officially signing them up in Her Majesty's waters. For now they would officially remain 'stowaways'. As the *Kearsarge* neared Brest on the coast of France, Winslow sent an officer ashore in a launch, together with the Irish recruits. Here the 'stowaways' were asked if they wanted to depart for shore, of if they would prefer to seek the captain's mercy. Naturally the prospect of being marooned in France without a penny to their name did not appeal, and all chose the latter course. They were officially enlisted and entered in the ships books 'for the purpose of their support and comfort'. The ruse was intended to circumvent any legal implications resulting from the recruitment, but it failed miserably.[168]

While Captain Winslow began to learn of the diplomatic disaster he had left in his wake, he scrambled to put into action his fall back story that the men had crept aboard the ship and concealed themselves without his knowledge. Winslow wrote to Secretary of the Navy Welles on 7 December:

> A party of men, either by connivance of the crew or otherwise, were concealed on board this vessel on the night of her departure from Queenstown, the 5th ultimo. These men I learn were in expectation of being enlisted in the service of the United States after the Kearsarge had proceeded to sea, but found their mistake.

Captain Winslow turned the *Kearsarge* around and headed back to Queenstown. He claimed that he had been unable to return immediately following the men's discovery because he had been watching the Confederate cruiser CSS *Florida* in the port of Brest. On 7 December, the same day that Winslow wrote to Welles, the *Kearsarge* arrived in Queenstown to repatriate the sixteen Irish 'stowaways.' As was later pointed out in Parliament, the fact that all the men who were returned subsequently pleaded guilty to enlisting suggests that Captain Winslow was being somewhat economical with the truth.[169]

British and US relations survived the embarrassment of the 'Queenstown Affair'. Subsequent investigations found that neither US Consul Edwin Eastman nor Captain Winslow had been aware of the recruiting, although at least in Winslow's case that is difficult to believe. Eastman had been particularly lucky to escape censure, as his dismissal had been ordered if any hard evidence emerged to implicate him. A number of the men who had enlisted on the Kearsarge were brought to Cork and charged with violating the Foreign Enlistment Act. John Sullivan, John Murphy, Edward Pyburne, Thomas Murphy and Denis Leary appeared before the court, the first men ever to be charged with breaching the Act. The judge and attorney-general gave lengthy speeches about how the young men had been led astray, and cautioned that they had no business fighting in a war where Irishmen's 'bones were bleaching under a foreign sun, where they had been entrapped by the hope of reward and by enormous promises.' All the accused were released with a warning.[170]

There was one fascinating postscript to the incident, which suggested that Captain Winslow was somewhat disingenuous when he claimed

Irish emigrants in Queenstown awaiting passage to New York in the 1870s. It was the hope of getting to America that led many young men to the USS *Kearsarge* in the hope of signing on. (Library of Congress)

to have repatriated all the men in Queenstown. It had been reported to the authorities that one of those who had gone aboard the *Kearsarge* was Michael Ahern, who had worked as a clerk at Messrs Scott in Queenstown until he had been fired, just before the arrival of the sloop of war in port. Although he certainly left with the warship, he does not appear to have been among the sixteen men who were returned. It is known that Captain Winslow had been in particular need of a clerk, and as a result was apparently unwilling to let the man go. Ahern was entered on the books as a Paymaster's Steward, with his place of enlistment recorded as France, alluding to the charade Winslow had earlier implemented with the 'stowaways'. The man who on 2 November 1863 was wandering the streets of Queenstown in search of employment would achieve an unlikely feat just over six months later.[171]

On 19 June 1864 the USS *Kearsarge* caught up with the Confederate warship the CSS *Alabama* off Cherbourg, France. The *Alabama* was the most famous raider in the Rebel navy, and had been responsible for the destruction and capture of dozens of Union merchant vessels since late 1862. The *Kearsarge* cleared her decks for action as the two sloops of war prepared for a fight to the death. Sand was spread across the forecastle and gun deck to soak up any blood that might cause the crew to slip while working their guns.

The *Alabama* fired first, at a range of 1,200 yards, but missed. At 1,000 yards the two ships started to circle each other, firing broadside after broadside at their adversaries. John Dempsey, who had chatted amiably to family friends at Queenstown, was struck by flying shards of metal, mangling his right arm beyond recognition – what remained would soon be removed by the ship's doctor. After forty-five minutes of action the *Kearsarge* began to gain a distinct advantage, and soon the *Alabama* had no option but to try and run. However, there would be no escape. The *Kearsarge* intercepted the stricken raider, and after a further exchange of fire the Rebels surrendered. All told, the battle had lasted an hour. As the Confederates scrambled to get off their doomed vessel, the *Alabama* sank beneath the waves.[172]

The victory of the *Kearsarge* was celebrated throughout the North, and the men on board were rewarded for their part in it. No fewer than seventeen of the crew received the Medal of Honor for their actions. One of the recipients was Paymaster's Steward Michael Ahern. On 31 December 1864, just over a year after he had been illegally recruited at Queenstown, Ahern was presented with the award. His citation read:

> Served on board the USS *Kearsarge* when she destroyed the Alabama off Cherbourg, France, 19 June 1864. Carrying out his duties courageously, PmS. Ahern exhibited marked coolness and good conduct and was highly recommended by his divisional officer for gallantry under enemy fire.

Unfortunately a transcription error has led to Ahern being officially recorded under the name 'Aheam' in the listings of Medal of Honor recipients. His story of illegal recruitment and subsequent heroism in action is perhaps the most intriguing aspect of the entire Queenstown Affair, which for a few weeks in late 1863 caused such diplomatic strain between Britain and the United States.[173]

The Civil War with canvas and camera

For four years the American Civil War was the major news event in America. Those on the home front were hungry for the latest details on how their armies were faring, and they expected to be speedily informed of major events on the battlefield. In order to satisfy this demand, forces such as the Union Army of the Potomac were accompanied by legions of correspondents, who reported back to their respective newspapers and magazines as soon as any newsworthy event occurred. Aside from simply reading the news, people were also eager to visualise the great battlefields and incidents of the war. To provide for this, Special Artists and photographers also journeyed with the armies, attempting to capture the look and feel of the conflict. Special Artists often sought to portray key moments on the campaign or battlefield, designed for reproduction in publications such as *Harper's Weekly*. The photographers usually produced their images for exhibition or sale. When photographs of the dead of Antietam were displayed in New York in 1862, it was the first time civilians had ever seen the cold reality of what death in the war looked like. The *New York Times* wrote: 'If he [Mathew Brady, the exhibitor] has not brought bodies and laid them in our dooryards and along the streets, he has done something very like it.' Two of the very finest proponents of Civil War artistry and photography were Arthur Lumley and Timothy O'Sullivan. Although the men themselves remain obscure, some of their work ranks among the best known of the American Civil War.[174]

The *Harper's Weekly* issue of 3 June 1865 sought to explain to its readers the role the Special Artists had played during the Civil War:

> The soldiers are marching home, and with them the noble army of artists. There never was a war before of which the varying details, the striking picturesque scenes, the sieges, charges, and battles by land and sea have been presented to the eye of the world by the most skilful and devoted artists. They have made the weary marches and the dangerous voyages. They have shared the soldiers' fare; they have ridden and waded, and climbed and floundered, always trusting in lead pencils and keeping their paper dry. When the battle began, they were there.[175]

'The Civil War photographer and his Kit'. Photograph taken by Timothy O'Sullivan at Manassas, July 1862. (Library of Congress)

Arthur Lumley was one of the very first of these artists. He was born in Dublin in 1837 and emigrated to the United States at a young age. Settling in Brooklyn, New York, he entered the National Academy of Design in the 1850s to study art. At the age of twenty-one he was naturalised as an American citizen. His first paid artist work was in illustrating books, and he spent the pre-war years engaged in illustrations for titles such

The Sacking of Fredericksburg by Union troops as sketched by Arthur Lumley in December 1862. (Library of Congress)

as *The Life and Adventures of Kit Carson* and *Wild Life: Adventure of the Frontier*.[176]

With the outbreak of the Civil War Lumley went to work for *Frank Leslie's Illustrated Newspaper*. As one of the most popular magazines in circulation, it insured that Lumley's work would have a wide viewership. In April of 1861 Leslie sent the artist to Washington DC, where he became the first Special Artist to be attached to what later became the Army of the Potomac. He was an eyewitness to the first major battle of the war, at Bull Run, Virginia, and he produced a number of sketches showing the initial Union success and their eventual retreat. By 1862 Arthur had moved on to the *New York Illustrated News*, who would publish no fewer than 298 of the Irishman's wartime illustrations.[177]

The life of a Special Artist was not an easy one. They experienced many of the hardships of frontline troops, and during battle had to sketch the action as quickly as possible. They often received no credit for their published images, which could be significantly altered and adapted prior to release. Arthur Lumley was present on some of the bloodiest battlefields of the war, such as Antietam and Fredericksburg. Aside from busily sketching events as they unfolded he also sent back reports of what he had seen, which helped the illustrated papers to communicate to their readers the particulars of the war. There was no guarantee that the work Lumley often risked his life to produce would end up being published, and in some cases it never even made it as far as his editor's desk. Brigadier-General Alpheus S. Williams commanded a division in the Twelfth Corps of the Army of the Potomac during the Chancellorsville Campaign of 1863. As his troops crossed the Rapidan River he encountered Lumley:

> We pitched a tent or two for headquarters and had the honor of finding two stray reporters of the Herald (Carpenter and Buckingham) and one artist of some illustrated newspaper (Lumley), which, said artist, by the way, drew some very pretty sketches of our crossing the Rappahannock and fording the Rapidan, all of which he lost with his portfolio before reaching Chancellorsville.[178]

Whatever difficulties Arthur Lumley encountered on campaign, they paled in comparison to the challenges that his compatriot, Timothy O'Sullivan, faced as he chased after the armies with his heavy and ungainly photographic equipment. The most famous practitioners of the art from the Civil War era remain Irish-American Mathew Brady and Scotsman Alexander Gardner. However, many of the most famous photographs taken during the conflict were captured by O'Sullivan, and they remain some of the most recognisable and emotive images of the war.

Timothy O'Sullivan was born in Ireland around 1840 to Jeremiah and Ann O'Sullivan. He emigrated to the United States in 1842 along with his parents, brother and sister. There is little known about his early life in America, although it is thought that he may have worked for Mathew Brady from a young age, learning the skills of photography along the way. When Alexander Gardner went to Washington DC to run Brady's studio there, O'Sullivan went with him.[179]

With the outbreak of war in 1861 Mathew Brady recognised the potential for photographing the conflict. Brady brought his camera to Bull Run, to capture early images of the fighting. Timothy O'Sullivan may have been with him on this trip – *Harper's Weekly* suggested he was when it later stated that the battlefield would have been captured 'close-up' but for a Rebel shell destroying O'Sullivan's camera. As it became apparent that the fighting would drag on, the Irishman was sent to locations such as South Carolina where he took photographs with Union armies in the field. In 1862 Alexander Gardner ended his association with Brady to strike out on his own. One of the reasons for this seems to be the fact that Brady often failed to credit his photographers for their work, instead listing them as 'Photo by Brady.' Timothy O'Sullivan decided to leave with Gardner, and he worked with the Scotsman for the remainder of the war.[180]

Timothy O'Sullivan would follow the Army of the Potomac for three years between 1862 and 1865. He travelled around in a small canvas-

Pickets examining passes by Arthur Lumley, drawn in Fredericksburg, Virginia, December 1862. (Library of Congress)

covered carriage, which served as both his darkroom and his home. Where his carriage could not travel he might take a small tent to serve in its stead. The process he used to take his photographs was called the 'wet-plate' technique. Once O'Sullivan had identified a composition he wanted to photograph he would duck under cover to coat a clear glass plate with a sticky chemical substance known as collodion. This wet plate was placed in his camera, the photograph was exposed, and the plate brought back to his portable darkroom to fix, wash and develop the image. The laborious process was not made any easier by the large and unwieldy camera which was the key component in the entire process.[181]

It was while working with Gardner in July 1863 that O'Sullivan captured some of his most famous images. That month they were the

'Dead Confederate soldier at sharpshooter's position in Devil's Den' taken by Timothy O'Sullivan on the Gettysburg battlefield in July 1863. (Library of Congress)

first photographers on the Gettysburg battlefield, taking their first photos on 5 July, only two days after the battle ended. Alexander Gardner had even been briefly taken prisoner by the retreating Rebels at Emmitsburg, Maryland, as he rushed to the scene of the fighting. Two of Timothy O'Sullivan's images at Gettysburg remain among his most well-known. The first, entitled 'Dead Confederate soldier at sharpshooter's position in Devil's Den' shows a dead Rebel lying behind a stone wall constructed between two boulders, with Little Round Top in the distance. The other, commonly known as 'A Harvest of Death' shows a field scattered with the bloated corpses of Union dead, still lying where they fell during the fighting. Research by historian William A. Frassanito has established that the iconic sharpshooter photograph was in fact set up by O'Sullivan and Gardner. It was common practice at the time to add to a potential image to improve a composition, and in this case the dead Rebel appears to have been strategically located behind the wall, as he appears in a number of other photographs taken in different locations.

While on the battlefield O'Sullivan came across one of his counterparts, Special Artist Alfred R. Waud, who was working for *Harper's Weekly*. He took the opportunity to capture his image as he sketched one of his fighting scenes.[182]

Timothy continued to capture unique images throughout the remainder of the war. He climbed into a belfry to shoot Ulysses S. Grant's meeting with his staff at Massaponax Church during the critical 1864 Overland Campaign, as troops filed past in the background. He was at the siege of Petersburg to record the conflict as it descended into something very similar to the trench-warfare more commonly associated with the First World War's Western Front. In April 1865 he was the first photographer to arrive at the McLean residence at Appomattox Court House, where only a short time before Robert E. Lee had surrendered the Army of Northern Virginia to Grant. Although he missed the main event, he photographed members of the family sitting on the steps of the residence where history had just been made.[183]

Arthur Lumley and Timothy O'Sullivan both went on to have relatively successful post-war careers. Lumley enjoyed a productive career as an artist, working for publications such as *Harper's Weekly, London Illustrated News, La Monde Illustrate* and *Fine Arts*. In later life he turned to painting, particularly landscapes and portraits and was a founding member of the Society of American Painters in Water Colors. When Alexander Gardner published his *Photographic Sketch Book of the Civil War* in 1866, many of the images were credited to Timothy O'Sullivan.

'A Harvest of Death'. Dead Union soldiers on the Gettysburg battlefield, taken by Timothy O'Sullivan in July 1863. (Library of Congress)

Between 1867 and 1869 he participated in Clarence King's geological survey of the fortieth parallel as the official photographer. The mission was to document the territory between the Rocky and Sierra Nevada Mountains, extremely challenging terrain for a photographer. He followed this with a journey to the jungles of Panama as part of the Darién Survey Expedition of 1870, before returning to the West in the 1870s to participate in the Wheeler Survey to explore west of the one hundredth meridian, which included areas such as eastern Nevada and Arizona; during this period he also visited Colorado and New Mexico. Among his most notable work at the time would be the many photographs he took of Native-Americans as their way of life became increasingly threatened.[184]

Tragically, neither Arhur Lumley nor Timothy O'Sullivan had happy ends to their lives. As the years passed cataracts developed over Lumley's eyes, causing him to lose his sight around 1890. The disability prevented him from earning a living. It was a sign of the esteem in which he was held that an exhibition of pictures was prepared in New York for his benefit, with paintings sent from London and Paris to be sold for him. The *New York Herald-Tribune* remarked that 'The exhibition will be one of the principal events of the season in the art world. Deep sympathy for Mr. Lumley is felt everywhere.' Arthur Lumley spent his final years living in Brooklyn before moving to the Mary Fisher Home in Mount Vernon, where he died at the age of seventy-five on 27 September 1912. He survived Timothy O'Sullivan by four decades. O'Sullivan had returned to New York in 1875, and bought a plot of land on Staten Island, but he never built a house there. It may have been that he planned to live there with his wife who later passed away. In 1880 he took a position as official photographer for the US Treasury Department, but had to resign after only five months, when illness forced him to move to his father's home in West Brighton, Staten Island. He was suffering from tuberculosis, which finally took his life on 14 January 1882 at the age of only forty-two.[185]

Despite the tribulations of their final years, and the few details we have about their lives, both Arthur Lumley and Timothy O'Sullivan left a legacy of work that still provide us with some of our most detailed windows into the American Civil War. Many of their compositions retain all the impact they possessed when first produced. Where much of the Special Artist's work transmits to the viewer the movement, scale and excitement of the war's key moments that of the photographer strips away the romanticism, presenting the undistilled realities of industrial war, down to the bloodied and bloated corpses of its dead.

Jennie Hodgers and Albert Cashier

On 6 August 1862 a nineteen-year-old Irish farmer decided to enlist in the Union Army in Belvidere, Illinois. He was described as 5ft 3ins in height, with auburn hair, blue eyes and a light complexion. His name was Albert D.J. Cashier, and for the next three years he would fight as a private in Company G of the 95th Illinois Infantry. When Albert mustered out of the service on 17 August 1865 he was a veteran of some of the toughest campaigns in the Western Theater, including Vicksburg and Atlanta. Albert went on to live a long and healthy life in Saunemin, Illinois, after the war. It was not until the twentieth century that an accident led to a medical exam, revealing the veteran's amazing secret – Albert Cashier was a woman.[186]

Albert Cashier was born with the name Jennie Hodgers in Clogherhead, Co. Louth, in 1843. She emigrated to the United States, possibly as a stowaway, sometime before the outbreak of the Civil War. A number of versions as to why she chose to dress and act as a man exist. One is that her uncle secured her a job in an all-male shoe factory on her arrival in America, and that she began to dress in male attire to secure the position. A former comrade in the 95th claimed that Albert Cashier told him the reason in later years:

Lots of boys enlisted under the wrong name. So did I. The country needed men, and I wanted excitement. I worked on an Illinois farm as a man the year before the war. I wasn't discovered and thought I'd try my luck in the service.

Whatever the cause of her creation of Albert, Jennie discovered that life seemed to offer more possibilities if she discarded Ms Hodgers and became Mr Cashier.[187]

Corporal J.H. Himes served with Albert in Company G of the 95th, and was interviewed in 1915 to record his memories of the soldier. When asked if he had thought she might be a woman during their service he replied:

> I never suspected anything of that kind. I know that Cashier was the shortest person in the Company. I think he did not have to shave … Albert D.J. Cashier was very quiet in her manner and she was not easy to get acquainted with. I rather think she did not take part in any of the sports and games of the members of the Company. When I was examined for enlistment, I was not stripped and a woman would not have had any trouble in passing the examination.[188]

Corporal Robert Horan of Company G looked back to consider if there had been any signs of Albert's gender:

> We never suspected that 'Albert' was not a man. But we did think sometimes that she acted more like a woman than a man. For one thing, she always insisted on bunking by herself. And she did lote [lots] of washing for the boys – she used to wash our shirts. When the strangeness wore away she made a good comrade. She was a soldier with us, doing faithfully and well.[189]

Albert's old Sergeant in the 95th Illinois was Charles W. Ives. He also remembered his wartime comrade:

> I remember one time when our column got cut off from the rest of the company because we were too outnumbered to advance. There was a place where three dead trees piled one on top of another formed a sort of barricade. The rebels got down out of sight. 'Al' [Albert Cashier] hopped on the top log and called: 'Hey! You darn rebels, why don't you get up where we can see you?' Another time Cashier gained distinction by climbing a tall tree to attach the Union flag to a limb after it had been shot down by the enemy … Al did all the regular duties. Not knowing that she was a girl, I assigned her to picket duty and to carry water just as all the men did … One time, we went into barracks at what is now known as Camp Grant … All of the bunks were double, but over in the one corner there was a single cot. Cashier asked me if he might have the cot. I consented and thought nothing about it.[190]

Private Albert Cashier marched across Mississippi, Louisiana, Missouri and Tennessee with the 95th Illinois Infantry. It is remarkable that his true identity was not discovered on campaign; his secret must have been a considerable additional burden to carry through what was already a tough war. With the war's end there seemed no advantage to be gained by going back to being Jennie Hodgers. After spending some time as a laborer in Belvidere for two or three years, Albert moved to Saunemin, Illinois. He would remain here, living life as a man, for over forty years.[191]

In Saunemin Albert worked as a handyman and gardener around the town. Village boys sometimes teased him over his height, calling him a 'drummer boy'. Unimpressed, Albert supposedly used to shout back 'I

Private Albert Cashier (Jennie Hodgers) during his service with the 95th Illinois Infantry.

was a fighting infantryman!' He was proud of his wartime service, and was a member of the Union veteran's organisation the Grand Army of the Republic (GAR). From 1890 Albert started to receive a military pension for his wartime service as a soldier. It was not until 1911 that Albert was first discovered. While carrying out some work for Senator Ira M. Lish in Saunemin, there was an accident with an automobile which fractured Cashier's leg. When the doctor arrived to try and treat the injury, he was shocked to discover that Albert was actually a woman. Thankfully for Albert, both witnesses agreed to keep the news to themselves. The secret Albert Cashier had guarded for fifty years remained intact.[192]

Age began to catch up with the old soldier a few months after the accident, and Lish helped to secure him a place in the Soldier's and Sailor's Home in Quincy, Illinois. Albert was sixty-six years old. The Superintendent and physician at the institution were informed of Albert's circumstances and agreed to be discrete, but it was now only a matter of time before her sex was revealed. It was 1913 when the story finally came out, and it caused a media sensation. Newspapers across the United States carried the news of the veteran soldier who was found to be a woman. The *Democratic Banner* in Ohio described the circumstances to its readers on 6 May 1913:

> The woman has been in the soldiers' home nearly two years, and has always been extremely companionable with the other members. She has become enfeebled mentally, and her secret became known to the authorities at the home a few months ago, when male attendants attempted to give her a bath. She appealed to a female nurse and told her story.[193]

One reporter managed to visit the home in Quincy and meet Albert. He gave a detailed description of what it was like to meet the army veteran in 1913:

I had expected to meet an amazon. A woman who had fought in the death grapple of a nation and had lived and toiled as a man through half a century should be big, strong and masculine. And when I entered her hospital ward there rose and came to meet me, in her faded soldier's uniform, just a little frail, sweet-faced, old lady, who might be anybody's grandmother. She was so little and so gentle! She could walk under the leveled arm of almost any soldier in the home. Most of them were giants beside her. If she was ever five feet two, age and toil had shriveled her figure and bent her shoulders till she belies her record. Her hand-clasp was timid and her hand was delicate and small. Her brown hair had whitened. Her eyes were a faded blue. And her face was a face for a painter to dwell on. Half a century of sun and wind had bronzed that face, sowed it with freckles and seamed it with a thousand wrinkles. The razor had helped her disguise and had coaxed forth a film of beard. But there was no touch of coarseness. It was a sweet, kindly, pathetic face, compelling affection and respect.[194]

Even though the story of the female soldier Albert Cashier had swept across America, Albert remained unaware in the home that her secret had been exposed on a national stage. With her failing mental capacity it had been thought better to continue to address her as Albert Cashier rather than Jennie Hodgers. There was a danger that a media circus would evolve around the old soldier, as photos of her in her uniform and as she looked in 1913 were in heavy demand. Those in the Quincy home were quick to step in to try to protect Cashier. They were careful to always call the popular soldier Albert, no matter what appeared in the newspapers.[195]

Unfortunately Albert Cashier's final months did not reflect well on those who were responsible for the old veteran's care. In March 1914 Albert was transferred from the Quincy home to Watertown State Hospital, an asylum. His condition upon entry was recorded as 'no memory, noisy at times, poor sleeper, and feeble.' There was no sympathy to be had here for a life where half a century was spent living as a man. Cashier was forced out of male clothes and into dresses, an action which caused significant trauma. For the first time since at least 1862, Albert Cashier was once again Jennie Hodgers, but this time her identity had not changed by choice. At least one of her old comrades in the 95th had doubts about why Cashier had been moved to Watertown. Robert Horan wrote to another veteran of the regiment:

> I have heard from Quincy from Scott. He told me about they taken Cashier away from thare. He tell[s] me he was about the same when I see him Nov last. But in Jan a Cathlick Preast had been coming in to see him and it was through him he was taken to Watertown in Rock Island County. He says he think the[y] can keep him cheaper. Cashier has some money in his old home & it in care of I.M. Lish, the man he worked for & who broke his Leg with his auto & took care of him & then took him to the Home. The Preast have heard of him having some Money they don't care for Cashier. It [is] his money thare after.[196]

Albert Cashier, or Jennie Hodgers, passed away on 10 October 1915 in Watertown asylum. Other veterans of the Grand Army of the Republic insisted that the soldier be buried in uniform, with full military honours – the grave was marked with a veteran's headstone. Their wishes were respected, and the funeral took place in Saunemin, Illinois, where Albert had spent most of his life.[197]

Private Albert Cashier (Jennie Hodgers) in later life.

Recent years have seen the people of Saunemin move to restore the small house that Albert Cashier lived in, a move which helps to commemorate one of the town's most famous residents. Albert D.J. Cashier is one of the best known of the female soldiers of the American Civil War, but what is even more remarkable is that he successfully kept the secret until 1913. It is almost certain that the proud Albert would not want the fact that he was a woman be the main reason his name is well known today. The treatment he received in his final months was unbefitting a Union veteran who had served their country during the Civil War. His dignity was restored by his fellows in the 95th Illinois and Grand Army of the Republic, who buried Albert D.J. Cashier not as Jennie Hodgers, but as a fellow soldier, veteran and comrade.[198]

The Irish 'Florence Nightingales'

Jennie Hodgers was not the only Irish woman to go to the front. Many other Irish women also endured the hardships of campaign, as they sought to provide comfort and relief to those affected by the conflict. Some were Catholic Sister Nurses, working for orders such as the Sisters of Charity. Many though were lay women, who often went to war with their husbands and brothers, and ended up providing vital medical and support services to the men around them.

There are many accounts of Irish women being present with regiments at the front. William Watt Hart Davis of the 104th Pennsylvania Infantry recalled coming across a woman during an artillery bombardment at White Oak Swamp, during the Peninsula Campaign in Virginia in 1862. He remembered:

> An Irish camp woman, belonging to a New York regiment, made herself quite conspicuous during the action. She remained close to the side of her husband, and refused

to retire to a place of security. She was full of pluck. Occasionally she would notice some fellow sneaking to the rear, when she would run after him, seize him by the nape of his neck and place him in the ranks again, calling him a 'dirty, cowardly spalpeen', and other choice epithets. The flying shells had no terrors for her. During the hottest of the cannonade, this courageous woman walked fearlessly among the troops, encouraging them to stand up to their work. Her only weapon, offensive or defensive, was [a] large umbrella she carried under her arm. In one instance she shamed a commissioned officer into returning to his duty. She belonged to the Irish Brigade, and her stout person, full, red face and broad language betrayed her undoubted origin.[199]

At the Battle of Antietam Sergeant Charles Hale of the 5th New Hampshire Infantry also spotted an Irish woman with the Irish Brigade, quite possibly the same one who had been at White Oak Swamp:

As our first brigade was forming to relieve them [the Irish Brigade] we saw 'Irish Molly', of the 88th New York, a big, muscular woman who had followed her husband in all the campaigns, and he a private soldier in the ranks. She was a little to the left of their line, apparently indifferent to the flying bullets, and was jumping up and down, swinging her sunbonnet around her head, as she cheered the Paddys on. Our regiment was maneuvering for position at the time, and the bullets that passed the Irishmen were pretty thick, so there was no time for anything else, as we were moving lively, but the glimpse that I got of that heroic woman in the drifting powder smoke, stiffened my back-bone immensely.[200]

Nurses and officers of the Sanitation Commission in Fredericksburg, Virginia. Among one of Bridget Diver's many roles during the war was an agent for the Commission. (Library of Congress)

Perhaps the best known Irish woman who accompanied the troops was Bridget Diver, who was sometimes called 'Irish Biddy' or 'Michigan Bridget'. Little is known about Bridget's life in the years leading up to the Civil War, other than that she was born in Ireland and followed her husband to the front when he enlisted in the 1st Michigan Cavalry. The 1st Michigan became famed as part of George Armstrong Custer's

Michigan Brigade, known as the Wolverines. The reality of Bridget's life has become difficult to unpick from the myth. One of the most dramatic accounts of her time at the front is attributed to the Battle of Fair Oaks in 1862:

> Suddenly the Union line gave way and retreated in part, leaving the wounded exposed to merciless fire. One soldier, prone upon the ground with a shattered leg, raised his hand after the retreating troops. From the horde of fugitives dashed 'Irish Biddy', soiled by the bullets that had swept through her clothing. On her head rested a regulation army cap, fastened with the necessary feminine hatpin. Her hair had escaped from its confinement and was whipping about her face, that was begrimed as her clothing. 'Irish Biddy' reached the side of the wounded soldier – who was her husband. He was too feeble to help himself. The woman raised him to his feet and … she half dragged and half carried him across the battlefield. [Returning to the regiment] 'Irish Biddy' stood and looked at them. Her eyes were blazing with scorn. Pulling her battered cap from her head, and waving it high as she could reach, she shouted: 'Arrah, go in, boys, and bate the bloody spalpeens, and revenge me husband! Go in, and God be with ye!' Three thundering cheers for 'Irish Biddy' rang through their regiment as it plunged into the maelstrom of death.[201]

Although a superb story, this account cannot relate to Bridget Diver, as the 1st Michigan Infantry was not engaged at Fair Oaks. It may be that it is yet another account of the spirited woman who seems to have accompanied the Irish Brigade during 1862. There are other accounts that certainly relate to Bridget Diver's experiences. Her roles within the

1st Michigan and the brigade generally appear to have ranged from cooking and washing to acting as a sanitary commission agent, nurse, hospital steward and ward master. She is even said to have looked after the men's spiritual well-being, seeking papers and books from the Christian Commission on their behalf.[202]

As well as performing these roles, Bridget was not averse to picking up a musket when the opportunity presented itself. Mary Livermore, who worked for the United States Sanitary Commission during the war and afterwards became a well-known advocate of women's rights, said of Bridget that:

> Sometimes when a soldier fell she took his place, fighting in his stead with unquailing courage. Sometimes she rallied retreating troops – sometimes she brought off the wounded from the field – always fearless and daring, always doing good service as a soldier.[203]

Some of those who came into direct contact with Bridget have left a record of their impressions. Charlotte E. McKay, a Civil War nurse, recorded meeting Bridget at City Point, Virginia on 28 March 1865:

> Bridget – or as the men call her, Biddy – has probably seen more of hardship and danger than any other woman during the war. She has been with the cavalry all the time, going out with them on their cavalry raids – always ready to succor the wounded on the field – often getting men off who, but for her, would be left to die, and, fearless of shell or bullet, among the last to leave. Protected by officers and respected by privates, with her little sunburnt face, she makes her home in the saddle or the shelter-tent; often, indeed sleeping in the open air without a tent,

and by her courage and devotion 'winning golden opinions from all sorts of people'. She is an Irish woman, has been in the country sixteen years, and is now twenty-six years of age.

Charlotte went on to describe a conversation she had with Bridget regarding the whereabouts of a little horse that she had seen in her possession the previous year, which amply illustrates the risks that Biddy took: "'Where is the nice little horse you had with you at the hospital last summer, Bridget?"

"Oh, Moseby captured that from me. He came in while I was lying asleep on the ground, and took my horse and orderly. I jumped up and ran away."'[204]

Another woman who met Bridget was Rebecca Usher; she recorded the story in a letter home on 7 April 1865. It illustrates not only why Bridget was so beloved by the men of the regiment, but also indicates that she had made friends in high places:

> A few days ago I saw Bridget, who came out with the First Michigan Cavalry, and has been with the regiment ever since. She had just come in with the body of a captain who was killed in a cavalry skirmish. She had the body lashed to her horse, and carried him fifteen miles, where she procured a coffin, and sent him home. She says this is the hardest battle they have had, and the ground was covered with the wounded. She had not slept for forty-eight hours, having worked incessantly with the wounded. She is brave, heroic, and a perfect enthusiast in her work. Bridget said to me, in her earnest way, 'Why don't you ladies go up there, and take care of those wounded men? Why, it's the worst sight you ever saw! The ground is covered with them.'

'We should like to go,' I said, 'but they won't let us.'

'Well, they can't hinder me,' she said; 'Sheridan [the commander of the army] won't let them.'[205]

Despite the sketchy knowledge we have of Bridget, it is clear that she left a lasting impression on all those she encountered during the war, particularly the men of the 1st Michigan and Custer's Wolverines. For half a century after the war's conclusion newspaper reports and publications on women during the Civil War regularly carried Bridget's story, telling of different aspects of her wartime career, such as her narrow escape from the clutches of the enemy at the Battle of Cedar Creek, how she rallied a wagon train of retreating soldiers, and her decision to spend a purse of $300 given for her comfort on the men of her regiment. An 1892 article described 'Michigan Bridget' to their readers: 'She was Irish, with all the Irish characteristics as to features and form, and though she had a temper as warm as her hair was red, she was jolly and full of humor, which made her a most acceptable companion at all times.' It remains a mystery if this is an accurate description of Bridget's appearance. What is certain is that she was one of the most notable Irish women to serve at the front during the course of the American Civil War.[206]

Irish women did not only serve the Union. One woman who served the Rebel cause became so famous that she was known as the 'Florence Nightingale of the Army of Northern Virginia' – her name was Mary Sophia Hill. Mary had emigrated from her native Dublin and lived with her brother Sam in New Orleans, Louisiana. She worked as a teacher while Sam was an engineer. In 1861 the siblings had an argument. Sam left the house and joined up with Company F of the 6th Louisiana Infantry, a largely Irish regiment that would spend most of its war in Virginia. Mary was distraught that her brother had enlisted, as she was convinced that he wasn't cut out to be a soldier. She decided to follow the regiment to the front and attach herself to the unit's medical staff so that she could look after him.[207]

A casualty area at Savage Station, Virginia, in 1862. Women such as Bridget Diver and Mary Sophia Hill spent much of their time nursing the wounded at the front. (Library of Congress)

Mary soon found herself facing the realities of war as casualties began to stream in following the first battle of Manassas, where she helped to deal with the wounded. Her diary records her thoughts:

> I remembered being asked by some to pick minié balls out of their legs and arms, while they waited their turn of the

doctors, who of course had to attend to the most serious cases first. They have not half supplies. I tore down all the window blinds, and rolled them into bandages; nor was there half hospital accommodations. I made good chicken-soup, and flew around generally. The sights of the wounded were fearful to look at; I was nearly wild with excitement, thinking, as each batch of wounded arrived, I might see my brother, or my Louisiana friends of Walker's Brigade.[208]

Thankfully for Mary, her brother's regiment was not seriously engaged at the battle. As the war progressed, the Louisiana boys under her care came to call her 'mother' due to her attentiveness to their needs when they were sick and wounded. Throughout she always found time to look after her brother, trying to make sure that he was well fed and clothed, while often despairing of his propensity for losing his belongings.

While Sam's regiment prepared to take part in Stonewall Jackson's 1862 Valley Campaign, Mary decided to travel to the Richmond hospitals to see what she could do for the wounded soldiers there. She soon learned that the 6th Louisiana were engaged and decided to rejoin her brother and his comrades. While en route, she heard a report that her brother had been killed in action, news which Mary describes as driving her 'nearly crazy'. Luckily the reports were premature, although Sam had been badly wounded. While nursing him back to health in Richmond, Mary also worked in the Louisiana Hospital, where she cared for many men of that state who were wounded during the Seven Days Battles.[209]

Aside from her work at the front aiding the soldiers, Mary had many other adventures throughout the course of the war. Availing of her British citizenship, she was able to move between Confederate and Union controlled areas, which included her home in New Orleans following its fall in 1862. This allowed her to carry out further compassionate work, such as bringing news of killed and wounded soldiers to their families and loved ones behind the lines. However, her actions did not go unnoticed by the Federal authorities, and in 1864 she was arrested in New Orleans and charged with 'having correspondence with and giving intelligence to the enemy'. At the time of her arrest she was recovering from scarlet fever, but despite this she was sent to prison for four months. She was eventually sentenced 'to be sent into the Confederacy as an enemy'. Following her ordeal she was never to fully recover her health, and after the war she sought redress for what she saw as unlawful imprisonment.[210]

One of the interesting aspects of Mary's wartime experience were her two visits to Europe, once in 1863 and again in early 1865. While there she took the opportunity to visit her family in Ireland. Her diary illustrates that the Irish experience of the American Civil War was not restricted to those who had left for America; she met an Irish family who gave her presents to take to their only son who was a sergeant in Company F of the 6th Louisiana, and a custom-house official who asked her to carry a letter to his brother in the war department in Richmond. One can only imagine what it was like for families such as these who had loved ones fighting at such remove from Ireland. Much of their time must have been anxiously spent waiting for scraps of out-of-date and often inaccurate information about the conflict.[211]

After the war, Mary was named the first matron of the Soldiers' Home set up by the associations of the Army of Northern Virginia and Army of Tennessee. She eventually moved to New York where she lived with her nephew until her death in 1902. The true impact she made on so many lives during the Civil War was revealed in a *Confederate Veteran* article written on the occasion of her passing. The magazine described Mary's funeral:

> Through the streets of New Orleans, at an early morning hour, marched a long line of aged men wearing gray uniforms, with bowed heads and saddened hearts. Before

them was borne the remains of a woman whom they had known in adversity, and honored as a queen among Southern sympathisers. The 'Florence Nightingale of the Army of Northern Virginia' was dead, and its surviving veterans sought to show their love and appreciation by burying her with military honors, an unusual and beautiful occurrence.[212]

Many of the men who marched in the funeral cortege had first-hand experience of Mary's kindness. One was John H. Collins, who had served with Wheat's Louisiana Tigers during the war and 'whose empty sleeve spoke silently of the past struggle in which he was a participant'. He bore a heart-shaped floral wreath of red roses, tied with a broad white satin ribbon. It was a final tribute from the men of the Army of Northern Virginia to the Irish woman who had made such a difference to their lives during the war.[213]

Aftermath

The consequences of the American Civil War reached far beyond the battlefield and the cessation of hostilities in 1865. Every soldier's death had a different impact, as families and friends at home struggled with their loss. Wives and children had to come to terms with the grief of their loved one's death, and also deal with the new financial realities that often accompanied it. Decades after the war ended many families were still affected by the Civil War. The same was true for many of those who survived the conflict, but who had been physically or psychologically maimed as a result. These men and their families faced a future that had been irrevocably altered by the events of 1861-5, and it was a future with which many struggled to cope.

As the war entered its final days in April 1865 an unexpected and horrifying tragedy struck, when John Wilkes Booth assassinated President Abraham Lincoln. The act sparked one of the most famous manhunts in American history, as Booth and his fellow conspirators were tracked through Washington DC, Maryland and Virginia. At the centre of these events was a Roscommon man, who despite having experienced many of the major battles of the Civil War, now faced his biggest task just as the conflict was drawing to a close. He was there when Abraham Lincoln breathed his last and was the man responsible for attempting to bring Booth to justice.

As the nineteenth century ended and the twentieth century began the number of surviving Irish American Civil War veterans dwindled. Commemorations became more and more important as these old soldiers gathered to remember former comrades and be honoured by younger members of the Irish-American community. Many veterans were extremely active in preserving the memory of their regiment's service, as they sought to publish their histories and construct monuments on the major battlefields. In doing so they helped to cement their place in the narrative of the American Civil War. They also provided later generations with the means to tell their stories, and created the memorialised landscapes that form an integral part of today's national battlefield parks.

Mingle my tears

The shockwaves created by the American Civil War spread far beyond the battlefields. Families with loved ones in harm's way lived with the conflict every day, facing the nerve-shattering ordeal of checking the all too regular casualty lists. In many cases their worst nightmares were realised. For those who lost a family member in the conflict, the Civil War would live on for years, even decades. It was particularly trying for a generation of Irish emigrants who had already borne the harrowing emotional cost of the Famine.

The Irish Brigade that encamped in 'Camp Winfield Scott' near Yorktown in April 1862 had yet to experience serious action, although soon the names of the fallen would be filling the New York papers. Despite the absence of the enemy, death could arrive at any moment, as it did that April for a member of the 69th New York Infantry. He was one of the brigade's first fatalities, but even in death he sought to ensure his family would learn of his fate.[214]

The soldier's death did not come as a result of Rebel fire, or an illness contracted in camp. His life was lost when a tree fell, crushing him. The careful man had made precautions for his demise. As his body was examined, a note was found in his pocket:

> My name is Patrick Casey, Co. B, Sixty-ninth Regiment N.Y.S.V. Any one finding this note on my person when killed will please write a note to my wife, and direct it as follows: 'Mrs. Mary Casey, No. 188 Rivington-street, New York.'[215]

Casey's death and the note on his body clearly had a profound effect on others in the regiment. Even though there was almost unimaginable slaughter and suffering to come, Patrick Casey was remembered as one of the first. This may explain why his story was retold in the 1867 history of the Irish Brigade. The body was carefully buried and the note he requested was sent to his wife. Patrick Casey was just another casualty, his wife one more widow, but who were they, and what effect did Patrick's death have?

Private Patrick Casey was not a young man when he decided to fight with the Irish Brigade. He was forty-three years of age when he enlisted in the 69th on 15 September 1861. His motivations for joining up are unknown – it may have been an act of patriotism or of necessity. When he marched off to war he left behind a daughter who was nine years old, Mary Eliza Casey, who had been born in New York on 5 March 1852. She was baptised in St Peter and Paul church in Williamsburg, Brooklyn, where family friends Patrick Dowd and Rose Farrell stood as sponsors.[216]

Patrick's wife at the time of his death was not the mother of his daughter; it would seem the Irishman's first wife may have passed away during the 1850s. By the age of ten Mary Eliza Casey had lost both her parents. Patrick and his second wife, Mary McCormick, had been married on 30 April 1860 in St Mary's church, Manhattan. They were four days short of their second wedding anniversary when Patrick was killed. Unlike her husband, Mary was illiterate, and so relied on intermediaries to assist her in obtaining the pension she needed to sustain herself.

It was necessary for Mary to prove that her husband had served in the army and that they had been married to secure assistance from the government. Among the evidence produced for her claim was a letter written by Captain Thomas Leddy of the 69th New York, who had himself been badly wounded at Malvern Hill and again at Fredericksburg. While still recovering from his wounds, Leddy wrote to confirm the circumstances surrounding Patrick's death:

New York, January 20th 1863

I hereby certify that Patrick Casey late of Co. B 69th Regt. N.Y.V. came to his death by the falling of a tree whilst in the discharge of his duties on or about the 26th day of April 1862, in front of Yorktown, VA.

Thomas Leddy, Capt. Co. B 69th Regt. N.Y. Vols.[217]

Captain Leddy's correspondence combined with a certificate of marriage was enough to secure Patrick Casey's wife Mary a pension of $8 per month. By now she was no longer living in the home she had shared with Patrick on Rivington Street, having moved to a nearby address at 223 Delancey Street, also in Manhattan. It may be that Mary was unable to afford the original rent in the absence of Patrick's income, or that she sought to move closer to family for support. In 1866 she applied for an increase in her pension as she said she was supporting Patrick's daughter Mary Eliza, who was still under the age of sixteen and therefore a minor. However, for reasons unknown, her request was rejected.[218]

There is little further evidence for the family of Patrick Casey in the records. It is not clear when Mary stopped claiming her pension, if she ever did so. His wife and daughter were the two central people in Private Patrick Casey's life, and he made sure they found out about his death. It was news they had to deal with both emotionally and financially in the years that followed.

Freshly dug graves at City Point, Virginia, in 1865. Each soldier's death often affected many on the Home Front, where families had to cope with a new emotional and financial reality. (Library of Congress)

Only a few days after Patrick Casey lost his life on the Peninsula, another Irish regiment was going into action nearby. On 5 May 1862 Lieutenant Patrick Hayes, from County Kerry, led Company G of the 37th New York 'Irish Rifles' into the fray at the Battle of Williamsburg, Virginia. As they charged towards the enemy Patrick and his men were also assailed by nature, as a severe rainstorm hampered their progress through a dense pine forest, which was littered with fallen trees. As the Irishmen closed to within 50 yards of the Rebel rifle pits a shower of lead was thrown at them by the waiting Confederates. A group of men crumpled to the ground – among them was their twenty-two-year-old acting company commander Patrick Hayes, felled by a fatal bullet to the heart. The young man was buried beneath a pine cross in Virginia and left behind a distraught mother, a young widow and a baby daughter. It was also the start of a pension saga that would span four decades. [219]

Patrick Hayes had emigrated to New York from his home in Killarney, Co. Kerry with his parents when he was eight years old. As he grew up in New York what had begun as a childhood friendship with Dorcas Monaghan blossomed into love, and the couple were married in St Mary's church on 15 May 1859. Their daughter, Ellen, was born on the 14 July the following year and was later baptised in St James' church. Patrick was a Fenian, and on joining the 37th New York in 1861 he expressed a desire that 'some good for Ireland would arise out of it'. Prior to the war he had been a 1st lieutenant in Welpley's Company of the Phoenix Brigade, an organisation established to provide military training to the Fenians. Just before his death at Williamsburg, Patrick had written to his mother to tell her that he was prepared for anything that might happen to him, having complied with all the duties of his religion and being resigned to whatever fate awaited him. Unfortunately for his wife Dorcas and daughter Ellen, that fate was death.[220]

Patrick's grieving mother wrote to the commanding officer of the 37th New York, Colonel Samuel Hayman, five days after the Battle of Williamsburg. She sought information on her son's death and the fate of his remains. His beautifully written response must have moved her greatly, as she submitted it to the newspapers for publication:

> Dear Madam,
>
> I am just in receipt of yours of the 10th inst. Your son, Lieutenant P.H. Hayes, was buried near the road leading to Williamsburg, and his grave is carefully marked, so that his remains can, at some future time, be removed, but at present it would be impossible. I endeavored to purchase a metalic coffin in Williamsburg, but none could be had there. I am now moving to the front, but I shall do all in my power to further your wishes in regards to the remains of your son. Allow me to mingle my tears with yours, for while you have lost your only son, my regiment has been thereby deprived of one of its most gallant officers, whose name will be revered by all who knew him, and who fell while leading his men in the thickest of the fight. The gallantry of Lieutenant Hayes and the brave men who fell with him, of the 37th, together with the noble conduct of the 5th Michigan, turned the tide of battle, and his name should form a bright page on our country's history.
>
> That God may sustain you in your sore bereavement is the ardent desire of yours truly,
>
> S.B. Hayman, Colonel, 37th Regt, N.Y.V.[221]

Patrick's twenty-two-year-old widow Dorcas now found herself a widow after less than three years of marriage, with a child under the age of two, and so she applied for a pension to support herself and her daughter. Their home at this time was 69 Oliver Street in New York. In June 1863 she was eventually granted $17 per month, backdated to the time of her husband's death. Dorcas got on with her life as best she could. She met Englishman John Marshall who brought added financial stability for her and her child and they married on 31 December 1865. With this remarriage her pension entitlement came to an end, as she now had other means of support.[222]

Some years later a new claimant emerged to seek a pension based on Patrick's service. In 1869 a thirty-year-old woman called Bridget Kelly became the legal guardian of Ellen Hayes, Patrick and Dorcas's daughter. Bridget had a right to claim for a pension on Ellen's behalf, as she was still a minor. Why Ellen was not being cared for by her mother at this time is not apparent, but Dorcas was supportive of the new pension application. Dorcas and Bridget knew each other, and it is likely that they were friends. Perhaps a change of circumstances meant that Dorcas was temporarily unable to care for her daughter. However, the pension claim began to unravel because of a mistake Dorcas had made on her 1865 marriage certificate. When she married for the second time her name was recorded under her maiden name 'Monaghan' rather than her name at the time, 'Hayes'. The government now asked her to prove that she was one in the same person as Dorcas Hayes, the widow of Patrick and the mother of Ellen. As a result of this simple error Dorcas had to organise a range of deponents who could swear they had known her for most of her life and that she was who she said she was. Finally in 1872 a minor's pension of $15 per month was approved, increased to $17 the next year. The pension was paid until 1876, when Ellen turned sixteen.[223]

By 1880 Dorcas was living in Queens with her second husband John Marshall. Ellen was by this time living with them, going by the name of Ella. John was a Dock Master, and he and Dorcas had three children, Clarence (seven), Dorcas (five) and George (two). There is no indication of what became of Ellen after this date, but John and Dorcas re-emerge in the early years of the twentieth century. They were now living at 744 Dean Street in Brooklyn. John fell ill on 9 April 1902, suffering from an inflammation of the heart. He was admitted to the City Hospital, but died eight days later on 17 April. Dorcas was now a widow for the second time in her life. Facing old age and struggling financially, she had little option but to turn once again towards the military service of her first love, who had now been dead for forty years.[224]

In 1904 Dorcas applied for the reinstatement of the pension she had received in the 1860s following Patrick's death. She was again tormented by the error on the 1865 marriage certificate to John Marshall, where her name was not recorded as Hayes. Dorcas explained to the authorities that at the time of her second marriage the priest had been informed she was the widow of Patrick Hayes, but 'through some inadvertence or mistake the name was omitted and the name of Monaghan only retained'. She had to renew her hunt for witnesses who could swear to her marriage to Patrick. In addition she also had to provide evidence that her second husband John had not served in the Civil War. Neither proved an easy task given the passage of years, and she had trouble tracking down people who could help her. However, Dorcas overcame these difficulties and she once again received the $17 per month that she had first been granted in 1863.[225]

After the passage of nearly five decades Patrick Hayes's wartime service was still providing for his now elderly wife. Dorcas received her last instalment of the pension on 7 February 1910. Almost forty-eight years after the Kerryman had fallen at Williamsburg the payment ceased; the reason Dorcas no longer needed it was explained on her file: 'Reported death. Date not given.'[226]

For Mary Casey and Dorcas Hayes the death of their husbands was just the beginning of a life that would constantly have the American Civil War as a reference point. They not only had to come to terms with the shock of their loss, but seek to quickly recover some financial stability in the absence of the family's main breadwinner. Young children such as Mary Eliza Casey and Ellen Hayes grew up having barely known their fathers. Theirs were stories replicated in thousands of other cases in New York and elsewhere. Until well into the twentieth century elderly women like Dorcas Hayes could turn to their forever-youthful husbands for assistance, a right the men had bought with their lives on the battlefields of the American Civil War.

The price of gallantry

The numbers of wounded in the American Civil War far outweighed the dead. Their plight is often overlooked, but for many hundreds of thousands of men the injuries they suffered as young men would deeply affect the rest of their lives. Among the most common fates suffered by wounded soldiers was amputation. Countless limbs had been lost to the surgeon's saw, resulting in severe impediments for men living in a society where the physical ability to work was the key to survival. For others injuries were psychological. The mental scars of the war often never healed, and many men and their families had to deal with the long-term consequences of the terrible fighting.

On 31 December 1864 Richard D. Dunphy was awarded the Congressional Medal of Honor. Then in his early twenties, the Coal Heaver had served aboard the USS *Hartford* during the Battle of Mobile Bay, Alabama on 5 August 1864. The *Hartford* participated in attacks against Fort Morgan and Rebel gunboats. His citation recorded that 'with his ship under terrific enemy shell-fire, Dunphy performed his duties with skill and courage throughout this fierce engagement which resulted in the capture of the rebel ram Tennessee.' Richard's reaction to his award is unrecorded. There was little doubt though that he and his comrades had endured a 'terrific fire'; Richard emerged from the battle having lost both arms following the explosion of a shell.[227]

Dunphy had enlisted in the naval service in New York on 18 December 1863. After the injury which had necessitated the amputation of the remains of his limbs while the *Hartford* was still in action, Richard was taken to Pensacola, Florida to begin his long road to recovery. A number of hospitals and many months later he was finally discharged on 21

January 1865. Although still a young man, he now needed a government pension to help support himself. He was provided with two artificial arms in the summer of 1865, but these proved to be of limited use as both of his arms had been amputated just below the shoulders.[228]

The indications are that Richard was initially able to get on with his life. On 11 September 1866 he married Catherine Cooper in Milwaukee, Wisconsin, a girl he had first met before his service. They decided to move further west, and settled down in Vallejo, California, where Richard would spend the rest of his days. The couple had fourteen children together, although only six sons and four daughters survived. Two of Richard's sons would eventually follow him into the naval service. On the surface the double amputee's life appeared to have become a success, but the injuries he had suffered and the dependencies it created were to have a devastating effect on the veteran and his family.[229]

Dealing with a disability on the scale of Richard's in nineteenth-century California was an extreme challenge for both himself and his wife. When Richard later sought a pension increase some of the difficulties he faced were outlined:

> … Dunphy has no use of either of the remnants of his two arms. [He] is totally unable to help himself either in putting on clothes or attending to any call of nature … He has no means whereby he could cook any food or eat or drink any food but by having the same placed near to his mouth and cut up or fed by a spoon … He requires wherever he is an attendant to prevent the soiling with filth of his clothes and person and that said attendant is necessary to clean him after stool and to save the filth from his person and clothes when making water.[230]

Richard increasingly turned to alcohol and gambling for solace. As he did so his relationship with his wife began to suffer. In 1874 he spent some time in a mental asylum, where the doctors 'thought that his mind was affected on account of the loss of his arms'.[231]

Richard and Catherine's relationship eventually degenerated to such a degree that they stopped speaking to each other, and in 1899 she attempted to have herself appointed his guardian in order to oversee his pension. She wrote that the family could secure little of Richard's pension money, which was spent in saloons and to pay gambling debts. Their twenty-two-year-old daughter Mary also felt that her father had a drinking problem which affected both the family's income and the way he treated his children. Although a subsequent investigation found that Richard did drink to excess and was argumentative when drunk, it also determined that Catherine had exaggerated Richard's problems, and her request for guardianship was denied. For his part, the old sailor strongly denied treating his family badly or failing to look after them properly.[232]

Richard Dunphy's tragic life came to a close on 23 November 1904, when he passed away in his early sixties. His cause of death was recorded as dropsy and heart trouble. After his death one of the town's residents remembered how the veteran had been exploited by some unscrupulous individuals in Vallejo:

> I myself saw him on the streets of Vallejo drunk a number of times and remarked to Capt. Tinelli, who was then Commander of the Naval Post to which Dunphy belonged, that I thought Dunphy ought to have someone to protect him from the leeches that were hanging around him. The men with Dunphy would actually put the whiskey glass to his mouth and take the money out of his pocket and pay for the drinks. He always wore a cape and though he had no arms he was considered quite a scrapper when drunk and about two years ago was cut up so badly in a drunken brawl that he lost about a gallon of blood and was too weak to talk for some time.[233]

Richard Dunphy is a hero of the American Civil War, and he will always be rightly remembered for his gallantry at Mobile Bay in 1864. With all animosity forgotten in death, he and Catherine today lie together in St Vincent's Cemetery, Vallejo, along with five of their children. Unfortunately he was not the only man who spent decades coming to terms with the impact of the Civil War.

After the conflict, the National Asylum for Disabled Volunteer Soldiers was established (the word 'Asylum' was replaced with 'Home' in 1873 to avoid stigma) to aid those veterans who were unable to care properly for themselves as a result of the war. The homes were set up across the country in a number of branches and were designed to be 'neither an [sic] hospital nor alms-house, but a home, where subsistence, quarters, clothing, religious instruction, employment when possible, and amusements are provided by the Government of the United States. The provision is not a charity, but a reward to the brave and deserving.' They were built on large grounds and operated under a military structure. Each branch had a barracks, dining hall, hospital, cemetery and recreational facilities. Hundreds of Irish veterans of the Civil War relied on the home to provide assistance until well into the twentieth century. One of the earliest to do so was James Manning, formerly a private in Company C of the 17th New York Infantry.[234]

James enlisted in New York on 15 September 1863, and almost made it through the war unscathed. At the Battle of Bentonville, North Carolina on 19 March 1865, as he and his comrades fought the Confederate Army of Tennessee for the last time, he was struck in the head by a Rebel bullet. When he first went to the home on 12 December 1866 the 5ft 5ins former laborer was only twenty-five years of age. He listed his closest relative as an aunt living in New York. It was unlikely he realised that he would rely on the assistance the Home provided for the rest of his life. His records provide details of a torturous existence of admittance, discharge and re-admission. In April 1869 he was sent to the US Insane Asylum in Washington DC, probably due to problems caused by the gunshot wound to his head. He was released in March 1870 but returned to the home in July of the same year. Although he left after a few months, he was readmitted to different branches of the home a further eleven times, in 1877, 1886, 1888, 1891, 1896, 1900, 1906, 1910, 1913, 1914 and 1916. Aside from the initial treatment he had received as a result of his head wound, over the years he also suffered from afflictions such as heart disease and chronic bronchitis. James Manning left the home for the last time on 14 September 1920, fifty-four years after he had been first admitted. He died in Yonkers, New York on 23 July 1922.[235]

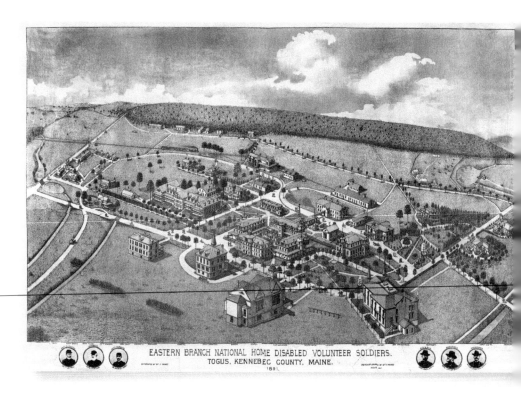

The Eastern Branch of the National Home for Disabled Volunteer Soldiers in Togus, Maine, as it appeared in the 1890s. This was one of the branches where James Manning spent time. (Library of Congress)

The majority of injured Irish soldiers lived out their days in the United States. However, there was a handful who chose to return to Ireland, and had the means to do so. The 1883 'List of Pensioners on the Roll' records ex-United States servicemen, widows and dependents that were then having their pensions delivered to post offices across Ireland. They were only a few dozen in number, but for some veterans it is probable that their decision to go home was dictated by the injuries they had received and the hope of support from family members who had stayed behind.

Some of these men returned with stories to tell. Peter Keefe had enlisted in the navy in New York on 12 October 1863, and while serving aboard the brig *Perry* he was part of the Union blockade fleet, designed to prevent shipping from entering and exiting the Confederacy. In late 1864 the *Perry* was patrolling off Murrell's Inlet in South Carolina, when a number of the crew, including Peter Keefe, were sent ashore to burn a Rebel schooner. Peter was captured by the Confederates, but decided that he would try to escape their clutches as soon as possible. He was spotted as he made a run for it, and was shot in the left leg. This resulted in the amputation of the limb above the knee. The sailor was discharged on 12 November 1864, and elected to return to Ireland, where he received a pension of $24 per month while living in Corloughan, Piltown, Co. Kilkenny.[236]

Two other pensioners who returned to Ireland were Corporal Louis Wilson and Private George Church, who had served in the 17th New York Infantry, the same unit as the luckless James Manning. It was a zouave regiment, which adopted a uniform with distinctive headgear, open jackets and baggy trousers inspired by French North African troops. Twenty-nine-year-old Wilson had originally enlisted in the 11th New York in September 1863, before transferring to the 17th that October. Church had also joined up that September, although he was ten years Wilson's senior at the age of thirty-nine. In 1864 the 17th New York was among William Tecumseh Sherman's forces that were driving towards

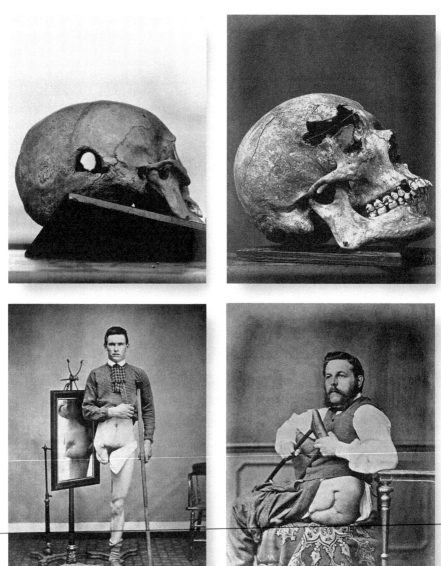

Above and opposite: War veterans. The reality of the American Civil War saw far more men maimed than killed. The difficulties of living with debilitating injuries often stayed with the victims and their families for the remainder of their lives. (Library of Congress)

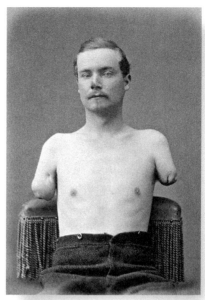

Atlanta, Georgia. As the Rebel Army of Tennessee sought to prevent the capture of the city a number of battles were fought, including one at Jonesboro, Georgia, on 1 September 1864. During the fighting Louis Wilson was hit in the right leg, and George Church went down with a wound to the left arm. As a result both men lost limbs – Louis his leg and George his arm. It is not known if the men knew each other during their service, but after their discharge both decided to return to Ireland. By 1883 each of the men was receiving a US pension of $24 per month. Louis settled down in Dublin, where he died on 7 December 1886. George returned to Cork, where he lived in Blackpool until his death on 27 September 1890.[237]

The consequences and cost of the American Civil War are perhaps no more stark than when viewed through the lens of those men maimed during the fighting. The war had taken their futures. In the space of a heartbeat their prospects had been transformed, and a life of hardship beckoned that would affect them and their families for years to come.

Hunting Lincoln's killer

At 8.30 p.m. on 14 April 1865 Abraham Lincoln arrived at Ford's Theatre in Washington DC to watch a performance of *Our American Cousin*. Just days earlier Robert E. Lee had surrendered his Army of Northern Virginia, and the capital was flushed with victory. The President took his seat in the Presidential Box with his wife, Mary Todd Lincoln, and two guests, Clara Harris and her fiancé Major Henry Rathbone. At 10.13 p.m., Southern sympathiser John Wilkes Booth stepped into the box behind the Presidential party. Levelling a Derringer pistol at the back of Abraham Lincoln's head, he pulled the trigger. The bullet penetrated Lincoln's brain, mortally wounding him. Major Rathbone reacted first, lunging for the assassin, but Booth stabbed him in the arm. He made his escape by leaping onto the stage, fracturing his ankle in the process.

He reputedly roared out *'Sic semper tyrannis'* ('Thus always to tyrants') before making his escape. For Major James Rowan O'Beirne, it was the start of a night he would never forget.[238]

Major James O'Beirne had seen his fair share of blood over the previous four years. He had been born in County Roscommon on 25 September 1842 to Michael Horan O'Beirne and Eliza Rowan, and was taken to New York when still a boy. He was educated in the city at St Francis Xavier and St John's Colleges, and on completion of his studies went to work in the offices of his father at Roche, O'Beirne & Co. James decided to go into business himself before the American Civil War interrupted his plans. In 1861 he enlisted as a private in the 7th New York National Guard, before joining the 37th New York Infantry, 'The Irish Rifles', as a 2nd lieutenant. By the time of the Battle of Chancellorsville in May 1863 he had risen to the rank of captain. During that battle a bullet ripped through his right lung and he was also struck in the right leg and head. At the time his wound appeared mortal, but he managed to survive. It was after this brush with death that he was promoted to the position of Provost Marshal of the District of Columbia, a position he still held in April 1865, when Lincoln was shot.[239]

After John Wilkes Booth's attack, the dying President of the United States was carried from Ford's Theatre across the road to William Petersen's Boarding House, where he was carefully placed in one of the rooms. As the Provost Marshal, James O'Beirne was in charge of Lincoln's deathbed and those who had access to the room. He later recorded the experience:

> I was officially present as provost marshal of the District of Columbia, with but short intervals of absence, too insignificant to be unaware of any important event which transpired in the room where the great Lincoln lay on his deathbed from the time when he was first carried into the modest house where he died, on Tenth street, nearly

> opposite Ford's Theater, in Washington … I was at or near
> Secretary Stanton's side, under his orders most of the time,
> and stood near him at the rear door in the gray of the
> morning when Mr. Lincoln died. He had been unconscious,
> manifesting life only by heavy stertorous breathing from
> the moment when he was first laid in the little rear bed
> chamber where he died. When first brought through he was
> more than comatose, hardly breathing. At the suggestion
> of the physician a civilian then in charge of him ran to the
> restaurant next door to the theater and procured a large
> sarsaparilla glass of brandy, which was poured down Mr.
> Lincoln's throat and seemed to re-establish respiration.[240]

O'Beirne recalled how Mary Todd Lincoln, utterly grief-stricken, knelt at the bedside and bowed her head towards the President's face. Despite the shock of the event the Provost Marshal had to remain mindful of his duty. When it became apparent that Lincoln would die, Secretary of War Edwin Stanton asked O'Beirne to travel to the Kirkwood House hotel in the city and bring Vice-President Andrew Johnson to the scene. James O'Beirne was fortunate that there was anyone there to collect. Incredibly, Booth's shooting of Abraham Lincoln had only been part of a wider plot that had been put into operation on 14 April. Secretary of State William Seward had been attacked in his home and stabbed by another accomplice, Lewis Powell, but Seward managed to survive. Meanwhile, George Atzerodt had been given the task of murdering the Vice-President, and had rented a room above his target in the Kirkwood House for that purpose. However, he lost his nerve and fled before he carried out the act.[241]

Having secured Vice-President Johnson, Major O'Beirne returned to the Petersen Boarding House and brought him to see Lincoln. Afterwards Stanton and Johnson had a discussion in the front room, and the Secretary of War began to dictate messages to foreign governments, informing them of the assassination. It was now the morning of 15 April, and Lincoln's end was near. O'Beirne was present when the President died, and the moment became seared in his memory:

> When Mr Lincoln breathed his last in a guttural, gasping struggle for breath, Mr Stanton was looking out of the window into the breaking twilight of morning dawn, with one foot on a chair, and holding its back with his right hand, as he leaned with his left elbow on his bended knee.[242]

The time was 7.22 a.m. As Provost Marshal, James O'Beirne was responsible for organising a manhunt to find the Lincoln conspirators. He first decided to return to Kirkwood House, where he discovered the room of George Atzerodt, the man who was to have killed Vice-President Johnson. In searching the room he discovered a revolver and ammunition, a bowie knife, a handkerchief belonging to David Herold (he had guided Lewis Powell to Secretary Seward's house) and a bank book belonging to John Wilkes Booth. The key find though was a map of lower Maryland – the neighbouring State to Washington DC. The hunt was on.[243]

On Sunday 16 April Secretary of War Stanton issued an order to O'Beirne:

> Major O'Beirne, you are relieved from all other duty at this time and directed to employ yourself and your detective force in the detection and arrest of the murderers of the President and the assassins who attempted to murder Mr. Seward and make report from time to time.[244]

The Lincoln conspirators had split up. John Wilkes Booth and one of his accomplices, David Herold, escaped Washington together, and as the map found in Atzertodt's room suggested they had fled into Maryland. James O'Beirne's men were hot on their heels. Members of his team

Wanted poster issued after Abraham Lincoln's assassination in an effort to track down the killers. (Library of Congress)

went to the Surratt Tavern in Surratsville, Maryland, where a John M. Loyd was arrested. After questioning he revealed that Booth and Herold had stopped there on the night of the assassination. The next stop was the house of Dr Samuel Mudd. O'Beirne suspected he may have been involved, and had jotted in his diary:

> Mudd, near Bryanstown. Son of William A. Mudd. A wild, rabid man. Served more than two years in the rebel army. Is a black hearted man and possibly was a conspirator. See after him.

Booth had indeed called on the doctor, to have the ankle he fractured during his escape from Ford's Theater treated. Meanwhile James O'Beirne personally led eight detectives to Port Tobacco, Maryland, where they arrived on 18 April. They discovered that conspirator David Herold had been there three weeks before, and had told friends he would be leaving the country. O'Beirne also questioned a widow who admitted that she was in love with George Atzerodt, who had also been in the town just before the assassination.[245]

Major O'Beirne was now convinced that Booth and the others had either fled into the Maryland swamps or were making for the Potomac River, with a view to crossing into Virginia. He met a detachment that consisted of men of the 8th Illinois Cavalry, 22nd United States Colored Infantry and 16th New York Cavalry. The soldiers searched the swamps, but found no sign of the assassins. The Irishman was now sure that Booth and Herold were heading for Virginia. O'Beirne and his men moved towards the Potomac, inquiring in farmhouses as they went. He recorded in his diary:

> Cob Neck is the whole section of land between the Potomac and Wicomico River. Pope's Creek has been a crossing. The conspirators are there if they have not crossed over to the Virginia side, which examine into and follow up.

Details then emerged that a man called Samuel Cox had been cooking provisions and taking them to men hiding in the nearby swamp; these men were John Wilkes Booth and David Herold. Cox's foster brother, Thomas Jones, had taken the assassins to the Potomac so they could cross into Virginia, which they did on 21 April. As the net tightened, O'Beirne noted 'send the men over to Mattox Creek and to work their way up and arrest Jones.'[246]

Now convinced that John Wilkes Booth was in Virginia, James O'Beirne crossed the Potomac with his detectives. Leaving his men,

O'Beirne initially pressed on in pursuit but soon returned, as his companions were 'tired out and leg weary'. The Provost Marshal's party re-crossed to the Maryland side of the river to report their findings and await further orders. In the meantime another report came in, suggesting that Booth might still be in Maryland after all. This new information caused the hunt for Booth to split in two; some men would have to follow up the new evidence in Maryland, while others investigated the trail in Virginia. Reinforcements arrived on the scene in the shape of Chief of the National Detective Police Lafayette C. Baker. He had reviewed the reports that O'Beirne had been making on his progress and used them to inform his own pursuit of Booth. Instructions were issued for O'Beirne to continue the search in Maryland – Baker would be the man to follow the Provost Marshal's leads in Virginia.[247]

On 26 April 1865 John Wilkes Booth and David Herold were surrounded in a barn on the Garrett Farm, Virginia, by Lafayette Baker and a detachment of men from the 16th New York Cavalry. The horse soldiers were led by Lieutenant Edward P. Doherty, who had been born in Canada to County Sligo parents. The confrontation that ensued led to Herold's capture and the mortal wounding of John Wilkes Booth. All the central conspirators had now been hunted down. The man who had stabbed Secretary Seward, Lewis Powell, had been captured in Washington on 17 April, while the Vice-President's would-be assassin George Atzerodt was arrested in Maryland on the 20th of the month. They would now pay the ultimate price for their crimes. On 7 July 1865 Herold, Powell and Atzerodt were hanged along with Mary Surratt, who had owned the boarding house were the conspirators had met before the assassination.[248]

James Rowan O'Beirne had not been there when John Wilkes Booth had finally been tracked down. Having led the chase for so long, it must have been difficult for the major not to have witnessed the final moment of the drama. Although Baker had taken the ultimate glory of Booth's capture, Secretary of War Stanton was well aware of the key part O'Beirne had played in the manhunt:

Four of the Lincoln conspirators; Mary Surratt, Lewis Payne, David Herold and George Atzerodt on the gallows on the day of their execution in 1865. (Library of Congress)

You have done your duty nobly and you have the satisfaction of knowing that if you did not succeed in capturing Booth, it was, at all events, certainly the information which you gave that led to it.[249]

The Provost Marshal received a small portion of the reward money that had been offered for the capture of those involved in killing Lincoln. He was also breveted a brigadier-general of volunteers for gallant and meritorious services on 26 September 1865. In the aftermath of the Lincoln assassination James O'Beirne went on to enjoy an exceptional and varied career. He studied law, became the Assistant United States Marshal of Washington DC and later served as the Registrar of Wills. In 1879 he bought and edited the *Washington Sunday Gazette*, which he converted into a Republican newspaper. He spent three years as the Washington correspondent for the *New York Herald* and journeyed west to cover the Cheyenne War for that paper. Among his many other roles he became the Commissioner of Charities in New York, was responsible for the immigrants at Ellis Island and acted as Commissioner Extraordinary in the United States for President Kruger of the Boer Republic. His interest in politics and activities in the Republican Party led to him seeking elected positions, though he never succeeded in gaining office. On 20 January 1891 O'Beirne was awarded the Medal of Honor for his conduct nearly thirty years before at the Battle of Fair Oaks, Virginia, on 31 May and 1 June 1862. His citation read: 'Gallantly maintained the line of battle until ordered to fall back.'[250]

James Rowan O'Beirne never forgot the traumatic night of Abraham Lincoln's assassination and his role in tracking down his killer. In 1909 he was called on to address the Lincoln Memorial Meeting at the Metropolitan Opera House, as the last survivor of those who had been officially present at the President's deathbed. He read Lincoln's Gettysburg Address to the assembled crowd, in what was regarded as the highlight of the evening. The man who led the hunt for John Wilkes Booth died at his home at 352 West 117th Street, New York on 18 February 1917. He is buried in an unmarked grave at Calvary Cemetery, Brooklyn (Section 7, Plot II, Range 9).[251]

The passage of years

The soldiers of the American Civil War did not disappear in 1865. The majority were still young men when the hostilities ended, with the greater part of their lives still ahead of them. Fifty years after the conclusion of the fighting there were still many men left who had served in Union blue or Confederate grey. In the historical record we catch only fleeting glimpses of these men in the twentieth century, as their lives continued to be defined by the great conflict in which they participated. As another war neared, these elderly soldiers still remembered those of their comrades from the Civil War who would remain 'forever young'.

As the fiftieth anniversary of the outbreak of the conflict approached in 1911, the ten-volume *Photographic History of the Civil War* was being prepared for publication. It included many images that had previously lain unseen and unpublished. In 1910 one old veteran, William Silkworth, got an opportunity to view some of the shots before they went into the *History*. As he leafed through the images he came across one that showed a group of Union soldiers relaxing as they played cards and read newspapers. Silkworth was taken aback. He suddenly found himself staring at a photograph that brought him face to face with the ghosts of his past.[252]

In 1910 William W. Silkworth was living in Long Branch, New Jersey. Although he had been born in the United States, along with many of his friends he had served in an ethnic Irish brigade, Corcoran's Irish Legion. Now, forty-five years after he had left the army, he was looking at a picture of his old unit. Most poignant of all was the fact that seated in the middle of the composition was his younger brother, George, with whom he had enlisted on 23 August 1862. Shortly after the photograph was taken, George became one of the hundreds of thousands of men to lose their lives in the war. William described the emotions he experienced:

> In looking the pictures over, you cannot appreciate or understand fully my amazement and joy in discovering

that one was my old Company B, 170th Regt. N.Y. Vol. Why, I could scarcely believe my own eyes, so wonderful was it, that after forty-seven years, this picture should come to me. But there they were, some of them looking right at me, who had been dead for forty-six years – and there was no getting away from that picture.

Today I am a boy again, living once more with the boys, the old army life. There were about twenty-five of us, school friends, who enlisted together, at Greenpoint, Brooklyn.

There right in the front of the picture sits my brother playing cards (You will note that he is left-handed. We laid him away in front of Petersburg). With him is John Vandewater, Geo. Thomas and Wash. Keating. There is Charlie Thomas and all the rest as large as life. With the exception of two, I have not seen any of the boys for thirty years.

Some younger eyes then mine, say that they can see a figure in the background with a flag. If so, it must be me for I was Color Sergeant.[253]

For the veteran of Corcoran's Irish Legion this photograph was far more than just an image of a few nameless soldiers on picket duty. It represented memories of his brother and his friends from what must have seemed a lifetime ago. When he enlisted in 1862 he had been nineteen; George only eighteen. George died in the attempt to take Petersburg on 16 June 1864 – William was himself severely wounded only six days later, on 22 June, and he spent the remainder of the war recovering from his injuries.[254]

While William Silkworth's memories of his comrades in the 170th were aroused when he least expected it, in the twentieth century veterans still gathered formally whenever they could to remember their experiences, and especially to honour those who had died. As the years passed these gatherings began to grow smaller, as old age began to claim the

'In looking the pictures over, you cannot appreciate or understand fully my amazement and joy'. The reaction of William Silkworth on seeing this photograph of Company B, 170th New York Infantry, Corcoran's Irish Legion, forty-seven years after it was taken. His younger brother is playing cards in the centre of the picture, and was later killed at Petersburg. (Library of Congress)

Civil War soldiers. The passage of time only heightened public interest in such events, as was the case when surviving members of the Irish Brigade came together in 1912 to commemorate the fiftieth anniversary of the Battle of Fredericksburg. The *New York Tribune* of 9 December 1912 carried the news:

IRISH BRIGADE TO MEET
Veterans of Fredericksburg Will Celebrate Anniversary
The fiftieth anniversary of the Battle of Fredericksburg,

fought December 13, 1862, will be celebrated at the
69th Regiment Armory Friday night by a remnant of the
famous Meagher's Irish Brigade, which took part in that
engagement. Led by Colonel J.J. Smith, of Cleveland, who
was lieutenant colonel in the 69th Regiment during the Civil
War, they will review the present regiment. The following
night they will be guests at a dinner in the armory, at which
two thousand persons are expected.[255]

The armory of the 69th New York National Guard at Lexington Avenue
and Twenty-Fifth Street was a natural choice for the gathering, as that
unit traced its lineage back to the Civil War regiment of the same name.
The occasion attracted a lot of attention and began with the veterans
conducting a review of the young militiamen who were drawn up to
meet them. On the evening of Friday 13 December, the 33 'bent and
snowy-headed men' who represented the remains of the Civil War
brigade from 1862 inspected the young soldiers, beneath the flags
they had carried during the conflict. The colors had been presented
by prominent citizens of New York during the war, and one of those
citizens, Levi P. Morton, was still alive in 1912 to witness the old soldiers
march under them once again.[256]

Although many of the veterans still lived in New York, some came
from further afield. Lieutenant-Colonel Smith had travelled from
Cleveland, Ohio, to participate, while Lieutenant John McGrath had
come all the way from San Francisco, California. All of the men were
then over seventy years of age, but their desire to meet old comrades for
what might be the last time drove them to undertake the trip.[257]

The dinner that formed the centrepiece of the commemoration
took place in the Armory at 7.30 p.m. on Saturday 14 December 1912.
Some 2,000 guests filed in to take their seats as the 69th's regimental
band struck up 'Marching through Georgia'. This was followed with
a rendition of 'O'Donnell Abu', before the veterans came into the hall

to the strains of the 'Star Spangled Banner'. A host of prominent members of New York society attended the dinner to honour the men, and the 1912 colonel of the 69th, Louis D. Conley, served as the toastmaster. Beside each plate a sprig of green picked from fields around Fredericksburg had been placed to signify the green sprigs of boxwood that the men of the brigade had placed in their caps prior to the battle in 1862.[258]

One of the speakers at the dinner was Dr John G. Coyle, who recounted to those present the Irish Brigade's experience at Fredericksburg:

> The figures of the losses at Fredericksburg tell the story of the amazing slaughter. The Sixty-ninth regiment, within whose walls we sit to-night, had nineteen officers and 219 men going into the fight. Sixteen of the nineteen officers were killed, wounded and missing, and 112 of the 219 men, making a loss of 57 percent. The Union loss for the battle was 13,771; the Confederate but 5,400. The Irish Brigade was led by the brilliant, intrepid and eloquent Thomas Francis Meagher, who was wounded in the battle. The Sixty-ninth was led by Col. Nugent, who was wounded, his pistol shattered by the rifle ball which wounded him, thus saving his life. The green flag of the Sixty-ninth was missing after the battle and great anxiety was expressed for its fate, for the regiment had never lost a flag since it joined the brigade. The day after the battle the color sergeant was found dead sitting against a tree trunk. Near him lay the staff of the flag. Clasped to his breast was the green flag and through it had gone the bullet that struck his heart.[259]

The speech of Dr Coyle was intended not only to honour the veterans present but to accentuate the Irish contribution to the fight at Fredericksburg. The passage of fifty years had added much embellishment to the story. Thomas Francis Meagher had not in fact been wounded during the fight, and the tale of the 69th's flag was apocryphal – due to the severe damage the Brigade's green flags had sustained in earlier battles, the 28th Massachusetts were the only regiment to carry the distinctive green banner at Fredericksburg.

The event was widely reported in both the New York and Washington newspapers. The *New York Evening World* went so far as to name each of the veterans in attendance and publish their group photograph. Souvenirs such as cigarette cases were produced to mark the occasion and were available to those who had attended the dinner. The occasion provides an insight into how, by 1912, the memory of the charge at Fredericksburg had become the defining moment of the Irish Brigade's wartime experience, and would become the stuff of legend. The commemoration itself served a dual purpose. First, it allowed the veterans an opportunity to meet old comrades and remember the sacrifices they had made half a century earlier. However, it was also an opportunity for the Irish-American community of 1912 New York to honour these men, and at the same time remind the city of the sacrifice the Irish had made during the Civil War.[260]

It is hard to imagine what memories were evoked in the minds of the Irish Brigade soldiers at those 1912 commemorations. Many of the events of the war must still have remained vivid for them. As the years advanced, each passing decade saw fewer and fewer men left who had known the horrors of the American Civil War. By the middle of the twentieth century memories had faded still further, and only a handful of survivors remained. One of the very last Irishmen was surely Jeremiah O'Brien. Born in Limerick in 1844, he was still collecting a Confederate pension an astonishing eighty-five years after the guns fell silent.[261]

Jeremiah O'Brien spent much of his life in the state of Texas, variously trying to eke out a living as a farmer and labourer. He claimed that he had fled Limerick city when a boy as a result of trouble with the police. From there he travelled to Scotland under his mother's name, before sailing to New Orleans in 1861. Although he recorded that he spent all

Left to Right, Sitting—Thomas Ferris, Com. John F. Cleary, Capt. E. F. O'Connor, Capt. John R. Nugent, Col. J. J Smith, Capt. John O'Connell, Sergt. Laurence Buckley, Capt. W. L. D. O'Grady, Capt. Henry Bates. landing—Com. John A. Butler, John F. Cronin, Major John Dwyer, Lieut. Dennis Sullivan, Com. William Bem mingham, Lieut. R. H. Birmingham, Sergt. Richard Finen, Com. R. R. Ryan, Com. William Sullivan.

The 'bent and snowy-headed men', veterans of the Irish Brigade at Fredericksburg, who posed for a photograph in the New York *Evening World* during their reunion in 1912. (Evening World/Library of Congress)

four of the war years in the Rebel Army, the service for which he received a pension was his enlistment in Company K of the 1st Virginia Cavalry Regiment on 15 May 1864. The old soldier, who had been known as the 'Kid' in his unit and was well regarded as a fine singer in camp, described himself as 'full-blood Irish'. He did not have his pension approved until 1932, when he made his second attempt to receive support based on his increasing frailty. Even when his $100 a month finally became available Jeremiah O'Brien had a lot of living to do. Surviving his first wife, he married for the final time in 1943, when in his late nineties.[262]

On 29 June 1950 the *Dallas Morning News* carried word of his death:

> Jeremiah P. O'Brien, 105, was buried Wednesday, leaving only three Confederate veterans in Texas. The aged veteran of the Civil War died Tuesday night. Services were held

A Grand Army of the Republic (GAR) photograph of Henry Mingay who was the last surviving veteran of the 69th New York Volunteers, having enlisted in August 1864 as a member of Company D. Born on 3 December 1846 he died on 22 April 1947 and is buried in Grandview Memorial Park Cemetery, Glendale, California. (Joe Maghe Collection)

in Kirbyville, his home. He had spent much of his time in recent years at Buna. Born in Ireland, O'Brien came to the United States on July 18, 1861, landing at New Orleans, La. He immediately joined the Confederate Army. He often told of being with Robert E. Lee when the Confederate General surrendered at Appomattox. He was a retired section foreman. His widow, five children by a previous marriage, seventeen grandchildren and twenty-five great-grandchildren survive.[263]

214

A memorial obituary published by the *Beaumont Enterprise* on 29 June 1950 included a photograph of the aged soldier, under the headline 'Honored Veteran Passes.' Jeremiah O'Brien was among the last of the American Civil War veterans. These men had kept alive their experiences of America's greatest war into the middle of the twentieth century. Jeremiah may well have been the last Irishman to die who had actually witnessed the conflict up close. With his death the story of the Irish in the Civil War became a memory, one that would for evermore be told through old photographs and books, rather than from the lips of those who were there.[264]

Back to the stone wall

After the American Civil War it became important for soldiers of both sides to remember their comrades, and to preserve the memory of their actions. Veterans' organisations such as the Grand Army of the Republic (GAR) and United Confederate Veterans were formed in the North and South. Regimental groups also emerged, as men who had fought side by side sought to maintain a connection with those comrades with whom they had formed a unique bond. These veterans were often also committed to preserving the legacy of their regiment, and making sure it was accorded what they viewed as its rightful place in the annals of the war. To achieve this many old soldiers dedicated themselves to recording the history of their unit in print, or physically memorialising it on the battlefield. As a result, for fifty years after the war's conclusion a stream of regimental histories were printed and regimental battlefield memorials constructed.

Irish veterans were no different to any of their comrades, and they also sought to have their stories remembered in the post-war years. In the North, those who had served in ethnic Irish regiments had the additional motivation of demonstrating that the Irish had fought just as hard as the native-born Americans for the preservation of the Union. Anti-Irish discrimination continued in the post-war period, and

Survivors of the 69th Pennsylvania Regiment meet with veterans of Pickett's Charge in 1887, shaking hands at the stone wall they fought over at Gettysburg in July 1863. (*Brief History of the 69th Regiment*)

memories of the 1863 New York Draft Riots and Irish support for the Democratic Party were still fresh. The Irish community's wartime dislike for the Lincoln administration was remembered all the more harshly as a result of the President's assassination. Emphasising the achievements of Irish regiments helped to 'rehabilitate' the Irish image in the United States. It played an important role as the Irish-American community moved towards a greater level of acceptance in society during the latter part of the nineteenth century.[265]

The first Irish histories to appear came in 1867, when David Power Conyngham authored *The Irish Brigade and its Campaigns* and Michael MacNamara published his brief account of the 9th Massachusetts, *The Irish Ninth in Bivouac and Battle*. Histories of regiments such as the 69th Pennsylvania (1889), another on the 9th Massachusetts (1899),

116th Pennsylvania (1903) and the 9th Connecticut (1903) followed. In addition to these books a number of personal accounts emerged, such as that written by Father William Corby, *Memoirs of Chaplain Life* (1893) telling the story of his experiences among the soldiers of the Irish Brigade. All of these publications helped to strengthen the memory of the Irish in the war. Battlefield monuments were also a key tool in this fight for memory. In 1887 the survivors of one Irish regiment, the 69th Pennsylvania, decided to make sure that their sacrifice would be eternalised on ground that would soon become the prime memorial landscape of the American Civil War – Gettysburg.

The 69th Pennsylvania had certainly been at the centre of the action during the fighting at Gettysburg. On 3 July 1863 the men of the regiment were positioned behind a low stone wall on Cemetery Ridge, in the centre of the Union line. All had been relatively quiet until around 1 p.m., when a single Confederate artillery piece boomed out across the battlefield. Suddenly all hell broke loose, as a massive Rebel barrage began to concentrate on the Yankee line. Over 150 guns concentrated against the Union positions atop Cemetery Ridge. The Irishmen lay flat on the ground behind their stone wall as an inferno of shot and shell descended on them. One remembered that the air filled with the 'whirring, shrieking, hissing sounds of the solid shot and the bursting shell … striking the ground in front and ricocheting over us, to be imbedded in some object to the rear; others strike the wall, scattering the stones around.' They had to endure this torment for over an hour, before the guns finally fell silent. Now the men faced a new challenge. From the woods in the distance, somewhere over 13,000 Confederates under the command of James Pettigrew, George Pickett and Isaac Trimble stepped out to begin 'Pickett's Charge', the most famous attack of the American Civil War. The 69th Pennsylvania was to be in the centre of the maelstrom.[266]

Colonel Dennis O'Kane commanded the 69th at Gettysburg. As the Rebel horde approached, he turned to his men and told them to hold their fire until they could see the whites of their enemies' eyes.

The stone wall and monument to the 69th Pennsylvania Infantry on the Gettysburg battlefield. The monument was dedicated in July 1887 by veterans of the regiment at the location they defended twenty-four years before. (Brian MacDomhnaill)

He reminded them they were fighting on Pennsylvania soil, telling the men 'let your work this day be for victory or for death!' The 69th waited until the Rebels were only thirty paces away before firing a devastating volley into their ranks. Still the Southerners came on. The enemy flooded in and around the stone wall as the desperate struggle intensified. Fighting became hand-to-hand, and men used their weapons as clubs. Hugh Bradley of Company D went down, his skull crushed by a Rebel musket. Corporal McKeever admitted that 'we thought we were all gone'. Robert Whittick of Company C described how 'a fellow was taken in with men and I knocked him over and took him prisoner, and took him in over the stone wall. We were fighting both sides on the front and rear of us at that time.' For a moment it seemed they would be overwhelmed, but finally the Southerners began to pull back. It was the same all along the Union line, as the legendary charge broke against the Yankee defences in what would retrospectively be termed the 'High-water mark of the Confederacy'.[267]

In 1887 the 69th intended to commemorate their part in this famous battle at the new regimental memorial located on the site of their defence. The Survivors Association of the 69th Pennsylvania had raised the funds to have it erected, and had garnered donations from groups such as the Ancient Order of Hibernians and The Hibernian Society for that purpose. Together with the other regiments of the 'Philadelphia Brigade' in which they had served, they made plans to visit Gettysburg. To add to the occasion, it was also decided to invite the very men who had opposed them all those years before, and an invitation was extended to the veterans of Pickett's Charge to attend. The *Philadelphia Inquirer* provided information on the preparations that took place:

> The Philadelphia Brigade (veterans of the war) met at the hall Eighth and Spring Garden streets last evening and completed arrangements for the reunion to take place at Gettysburg on the 21 of July. Two monuments will be dedicated, by the Sixty-ninth and Seventy-first regiments, as

The fiftieth anniversary reunion at Gettysburg in 1913. Confederate veterans of Pickett's Charge are in the foreground, while Union veterans line the stone wall they defended in the background. (Library of Congress)

well as a tablet to Cushing's Battery, erected at the expense of the Seventy-first. Pickett's division will be present as the guests of the Philadelphia Brigade. The regiments to participate are the Sixty-ninth, Seventy-first, Seventy-second and the One-hundred and sixth, composing the Philadelphia Brigade.[268]

Shortly before 9 p.m. on 2 July 1887 the Confederate veterans from Pickett's Division disembarked from their train cars at Gettysburg. Nearly 500 men of the Philadelphia Brigade were there to meet them. Illuminated under red and green lights, roman candles were fired into the night sky as the band played Dixie and the Stars and Stripes were unfurled. It was a momentous occasion, the first time that organised groups of former Union and Confederate soldiers had met on the battlefield since 1863. One of the members of the 69th explained the reasons behind inviting their former enemies to the ceremony:

> We … believed that our victory would be fruitless if all the citizens of all sections of our country could not enjoy equal rights and privileges as guaranteed by the constitution of our country, and noticing that bitter hatreds were kept alive by unscrupulous and designing men, that sectional feelings were fostered which would tend to make disunion sought for, and again destroy that peace that the end of the war brought about, we deemed it a holy and patriotic duty to invite our late foes to meet us in fraternal re-union on that field that turned the tide of war and led to final success, and there set the example of burying, forever, all animosities.[269]

At noon the following day, 3 July, the veterans of the 69th Pennsylvania left Washington House in the town and marched to the stone wall they had defended twenty-four years before. They were accompanied by the other members of the Philadelphia Brigade, the Confederate veterans, Post 10 of the Grand Army of the Republic and the Hibernian Rifles, which had accompanied the Irishmen from Philadelphia to act as an escort and firing party. Arriving at the wall, the speakers made their way to a stand erected beside the new monument for the occasion, as the accompanying band played a dirge. Former Adjutant of the 69th, Anthony McDermott, was the first to address the assembled crowd:

> Comrades, you of the Blue and of the Grey, we have assembled here on this twenty-fourth anniversary of the closing of the battle of Gettysburg, to dedicate this monument in commemoration of the battle and as a memorial to our fallen comrades, who gave up their lives that the Union might be saved. It was here that you, my comrades of the Sixty-ninth, delivered the final blow that gave victory to our arms; that you met the then foe in hand-to-hand combat and forced him (with the assistance of the Seventy-first, Seventy-second, One Hundred and Sixth Pennsylvania, and other regiments) to give up the contest. We entered this fight with an aggregate strength of 258, and suffered a loss of 151.[270]

The next speaker was the first colonel of the 69th and later Brigadier-General, Welshman Joshua T. Owen. He started in stirring style:

> Survivors of the Sixty-ninth Regiment Pennsylvania Volunteers: I salute you as the veterans not of the battle of Gettysburg only, but of all the battles of the war of rebellion in which the army of the Potomac was engaged. In all probability the battle fought right here on either side of this historic stone wall was the hottest contested and the

most important in its effects of any conflict of the war. On this day twenty-four years ago there was seen to emerge from yonder woods a body of troops, whose fame has since rivalled that of any body of equal numerical strength in ancient or modern warfare. In a fit of desperate courage the foremost soldier of the rebellion dared to challenge fate itself and hazard, upon one venture, the success or failure of the cause for which he had risked everything.[271]

More speeches followed, building to a poignant moment when the names of those who had fallen during the battle were read out. Afterward the monument was officially handed over to the Gettysburg Battlefield Memorial Association. A presentation was also made by the 69th to Sallie Pickett, the widow of Confederate General George Pickett who had given his name to the Rebel charge. It consisted of a 3ft high trefoil of white flowers, representing the badge of the Second Corps, of which the 69th had formed a part. That evening the 69th entertained their former enemies in the town, sharing refreshments and cigars around a 'camp fire' set up in the gardens of their hotel. The next day both Union and Confederates once again walked the field, and shared stories of their actions during the battle. They posed together for a series of photographs around the stone wall and shook hands across the obstacle that they had struggled over during the war.[272]

The 69th Pennsylvania memorial was just one of the hundreds to spring up at Gettysburg and battlefields around the United States after the war. Increasingly there was a conscious effort towards reconciliation of old foes, though the Union men never wavered in also extolling the justness of their cause. Ultimately such commemoration acted as a focal point for men of both sides to remember the service of their youth, physically express the reasons for which they had fought, and honour those who had fallen at their side. These were the thoughts communicated by Captain Edward Thompson of the 69th after he mounted the podium during the 1887 rededication:

> Once more we stand upon this historic spot, not in contention with foes, but to help heal the wounds made by the bitter struggle of twenty-four years ago, and to erect hereon a monument commemorating our services, and as a memorial to our fallen comrades. Thoughts of our brave fallen companions have suggested the following few lines:

TO OUR FALLEN COMRADES

On this historic spot we miss full many
Of the light of heart who in our perils and our sports took
part;
They died here, for man was born to die;
For them we shed no tear, we heave no sigh,
But mark with admiration and with pride
How gallantly they fought, how bravely they died,
Is there he who worries heaven with a coward's prayer,
His life to ages, healthiness to spare?
Who begs this boon, on a sick bed to lie?
Of disease, inch by inch to die?
More glorious was our lost companions' lot,
To fall here where the battle raged loud and hot,
Bound to their posts on this crimson sod
Where freedom triumphed, to the breast of God,
Their last gaze fixed on starry emblem and flag of green
That waved in glory o'er this battle scene.
The last sound that fell upon their ears,
Were their comrades' volleys and their comrades' cheers,

Like them we swear to fill a hero's grave,
Like them to perish or the Union save.
For no hatred, no desire for gold accursed
Caused us to mingle in this war at first.
For human wisdom, human love,
Never planned laws like those above
A government so grand!
We shared its glories and its perils share,
And before our God who hears, we swear,
The stars may fall from yon blue vault of heaven,
But not one star from our flag will be riven,
Which o'er his troops when human rights were won,
Was waved by mankind's hero – Washington.
The earth may melt, the sun the ocean drain,
These laws shall stand, this government remain.[273]

Epilogue

I once found an old flag, an Irish Brigade flag which had been used during the Civil War by the Irish Brigade here in this country. He liked that very much, and we got it to give to the President of Ireland. He and Mrs. Kennedy spent a great deal of time deciding how it should be presented; how it should be framed, encased in glass, what the plaque should say. The President, being such an historian, insisted that the plaque tell the whole story of the flag. He made me check and recheck, and he said, 'That sounds fishy. Something's wrong with your facts. Get your facts straight.'[274]

This is how Letitia Baldridge Hollensteiner, White House Social Secretary to President John F. Kennedy, remembered the preparations for JKF's visit to Ireland in June 1963. It would be the first time a serving United States President would visit Ireland, and his address in Dáil Éireann would be the first occasion on which television cameras would be allowed to film an event there. Given the magnitude of the occasion, and the President's ancestry, JKF clearly felt he needed to bring an extra special gift.

The flag that Letitia Baldridge Hollensteiner had sourced was the second green color of the 69th New York Infantry, the first regiment of the Irish Brigade. By late 1862, the original colors which had been presented to the regiments of the brigade were in tatters, and badly needed replacement. The new flags were sponsored by New York merchants and consisted of one green flag and one national color per regiment. They became known as the 'Tiffany' colors, as they were manufactured by Tiffany & Co. Although they were officially presented to representatives of the brigade by Henry F. Spaulding in early December, they had not yet arrived at the front when the Irish Brigade made its famous charge against Marye's Heights, Fredericksburg, on 13 December 1862.

It is somewhat ironic that the new flags arrived in Fredericksburg immediately after the Irish Brigade had been effectively annihilated charging the stone wall. Indeed, after the battle the Irish appropriated the theatre in Fredericksburg to have a reception for the colors, despite the fact that the town remained under enemy fire. The banquet was attended by Winfield Scott Hancock, the Irishmen's divisional and later corps commander. He remarked of the occasion that 'only Irishmen could enjoy themselves thus.' The flags were returned to New York to await the Irish Brigade's return to full strength; however the unit was destined never to fully recover from the losses sustained at Fredericksburg. After the war, the 69th's green color was housed in the regimental Armory in New York, until in 1963 it was identified as the ideal gift for JFK to present to the people of Ireland.[275]

When President Kennedy finally gave his historic speech to the Irish Parliament, he chose to open by discussing the flag and the Irish contribution to the United States:

> Mr Speaker, Prime Minister, Members of the Parliament:
> I am grateful for your welcome and for that of your countrymen.

The 13th day of September [*sic*], 1862, will be a day long remembered in American history. At Fredericksburg, Maryland [*sic*], thousands of men fought and died on one of the bloodiest battlefields of the American Civil War. One of the most brilliant stories of that day was written by a band of 1,200 men who went into battle wearing a green sprig in their hats. They bore a proud heritage and a special courage, given to those who had long fought for the cause of freedom. I am referring, of course, to the Irish Brigade. General Robert E. Lee, the great military leader of the Southern Confederate forces, said of this group of men after the battle: 'The gallant stand which this bold brigade made on the heights of Fredericksburg is well known. Never were men so brave. They ennobled their race by their splendid gallantry on that desperate occasion. Their brilliant, though hopeless, assaults on our lines excited the hearty applause of our officers and soldiers'.

Of the 1,200 men who took part in that assault, 280 survived the battle. The Irish Brigade was led into battle on that occasion by Brigadier General Thomas F. Meagher, who had participated in the unsuccessful Irish uprising of 1848, was captured by the British and sent in a prison ship to Australia, from whence he finally came to America. In the fall of 1862, after serving with distinction and gallantry in some of the toughest fighting of this most bloody struggle, the Irish Brigade was presented with a new set of flags. In the city ceremony, the city chamberlain gave them the motto 'The Union, our Country, and Ireland Forever'. Their old ones having been torn to shreds by bullets in previous battles. Captain Richard McGee took possession of these flags on September 2nd in New York City and arrived with them at the Battle of Fredericksburg and carried them in the battle. Today, in recognition of what these gallant Irishmen and what millions of other Irish have done for my country, and through the generosity of the Fighting 69th, I would like to present one of these flags to the people of Ireland.[276]

At this point President Kennedy pulled back the curtains to reveal the 69th's Tiffany color. The Irish contribution to the American Civil War was of course a natural starting point for such an important speech by the President of the United States. The flag remains the most significant object relating to the Irish experience of the American Civil War in Ireland. Following the President's visit, the flag was hung in Dáil Éireann, where it remains to this day.

When JFK spoke to the Irish Parliament in 1963 it was 100 years since the American Civil War had been fought. He was fully aware of the Irish contribution to the conflict, and the effect it had on the Irish community in the United States. He was most likely unaware that it was a contribution that had at least partly been forgotten in Ireland, where a focus on the remembrance of nationalist struggles dominated in the twentieth century.

Although the twenty-first century has seen the welcome expansion of Irish remembrance to include those lost in conflicts such as the First World War, unfortunately the American Civil War remains on the periphery. The often remarkable stories of those Irish caught up in the conflict remain largely forgotten, and have thus far failed to capture the historical imagination of the country in a way that the First World War has. Neither is there a national memorial to the 1.6 million Irish men, women and children in the North and the South who were affected by what was a defining war in the history of the United States. This is a situation that will hopefully be addressed by the Irish State in the future, if and when the Irish experience of the American Civil War emerges from the shadows of Irish memory.

Notes

1   The figure of 150,000 Irish in the Union Army is widely accepted
     by the majority of academic historians. The latest work on the
     Irish in the Confederacy is the basis for the figure of 20,000. The
     1860 US Census records 1,611,304 people as Irish. See Susannah
     Ural Bruce, *The Harp and the Eagle: Irish-American Volunteers and
     the Union Army, 1861-1865* (New York University Press 2006),
     p.2; David T. Gleeson, 'Irish Rebels, Southern Rebels: The Irish
     Confederates' in Susannah J. Ural (ed.) *Civil War Citizens: Race,
     Ethnicity and Identity in America's Bloodiest Conflict* (New York
     University Press), pp.133-55; Campbell Gibson & Emily Lennon
     2011, *Region and Country or Area of Birth of the Foreign-Born
     Population, With Geographic Detail Shown in Decennial Census
     Publications of 1930 or Earlier: 1850 to 1930 and 1960 to 1990,*
     (US Bureau of the Census) http://www.census.gov/population/
     www/documentation/twps0029/tab04.html (Accessed 6 October
     2012).
2   David Fitzpatrick, 'Militarism in Ireland 1900-1922' in Thomas
     Bartlett & Keith Jeffery (eds), *A Military History of Ireland*, pp.379-
     406.

3　Ezra J. Warner, *Generals in Blue* (Louisiana State University Press, 2006), pp.444–5; William H. Condon, *Life of Major-General James Shields* (Blakely Printing Co., 1900), pp.10–29. There are a number of different birthdates given for Shields, ranging from 6 May 1806 to 18 May 1810.

4　Louis Vargo, 'Abraham Lincoln Prepares to Fight a Saber Duel', *Civil War Times*, February 2002.

5　Abraham Lincoln, *Lincoln: Speeches and Writings 1832-1858* (The Library of America, 1989), pp.96–101; William H. Herndon, *Herndon's Lincoln: A True Story of A Great Life* (Herndon's Lincoln Publishing Company, 1888), pp.240–3.

6　Abraham Lincoln & Roy Prentice Basler, *The Collected Works of Abraham Lincoln*, Vol. 1 (Abraham Lincoln Association, 1953), pp.299–300.

7　*Ibid*.

8　Lincoln, *Speeches and Writings 1832-1858*, pp.102–3; Francis F. Browne, *The Every-Day Life of Abraham Lincoln* (N.D. Thompson Publishing, 1886), p. 184.

9　Lincoln, *Speeches and Writings 1832-1858*, p. 103.

10　Herndon, *Herndon's Lincoln*, pp.255–9.

11　Warner, *Generals in Blue*, p.444; Condon, *Life of Major-General James Shields*, pp.55–69.

12　Warner, *Generals in Blue*, pp.444–5; for the best description of events in the Shenandoah Valley in 1862 and Shields' involvement see Peter Cozzens, *Shenandoah 1862: Stonewall Jackson's Valley Campaign* (University of North Carolina Press, 2008).

13　Stephen Cooper Ayres, *Sketch of the Life and Services of Vice Admiral Stephen C. Rowan, U.S. Navy* (Ohio Commandery of the Loyal Legion, 1910), pp.1–6; Official Records of the Union and Confederate Navies: Series 1, Vol. 4, p.234.

14   Official Records Series 1, Vol. 4, pp.235-6.

15   David Detzer, *Allegiance: Fort Sumter, Charleston, and the Beginning of the Civil War* (Harcourt Inc., 2001), p. 231.

16   Official Records Series 1, Vol. 4, p.235.

17   Official Records Series 1, Vol. 4, p.253; Detzer, *Allegiance* p.231.

18   Official Records Series 1, Vol. 4, pp.253-4.

19   Recent research has seen the estimate of fatalities as a result of the American Civil War rise to 750,000. See J. David Hacker, 'A Census-Based Count of the Civil War Dead', *Civil War History*, Vol. 57, No. 4, 2011.

20   Naval Historical Center Biography of Stephen Clegg Rowan (http://www.history.navy.mil/photos/pers-us/uspers-r/s-rowan.htm).

21   Ural Bruce, *The Harp and the Eagle*, pp.31-3.

22   James McPherson, *Battle Cry of Freedom* (Oxford University Press, 1988), pp.201-6; US Marine Corps Muster Rolls; Bernard C. Nalty, *United States Marines at Harper's Ferry and in the Civil War* (United States Marine Corps, 1983), p.6.

23   Fort Sumter National Park Service, *Fort Sumter's Garrison by Nationality* (http://www.nps.gov/fosu/historyculture/upload/FOSU-Garrison-by-Nationality.pdf accessed 19 Sept. 2012).

24   'Letter from a Soldier in Fort Sumter', *New York Times*, 7 January 1861.

25   US Army Register of Enlistments 1798-1914; US Returns for Military Posts 1806-1916.

26   Abner Doubleday, *Reminiscences of Forts Sumter and Moultrie in 1860-'61* (Harper & Brothers, 1876), pp. 145-6.

27   *New York Irish World*, 7 June 1809, 'The First Gun of the War Fired from Fort Sumter by James Gibbons'.

28   David Detzer, *Allegiance*, p. 304.

29 David Detzer, *Allegiance*, pp.306-9; US Army Register of Enlistments 1798-1914; Doubleday, *Reminiscences of Forts Sumter and Moultrie*, pp.171-2.

30 US Army Register of Enlistments 1798-1914; David Detzer, *Allegiance*, pp.306-9; Doubleday, *Reminiscences of Forts Sumter and Moultrie*, pp.171-2.

31 James H. McLaughlin, *James Haggerty of Tír Conaill: Irish Patriot, American Hero* (Donegal Association of New York, 1992); The 1860 Census records James Haggerty as a forty-year old carpenter living in the 1st District of the 17th Ward with his twenty-three-year-old wife Elisa and one-year-old daughter Rosina; John Gilmary Shea, *The Fallen Brave: A Biographical Memorial of the American Officers who Have Given Their Lives for the Preservation of the Union* (C.B. Richardson & Co., 1861).

32 Wisconsin Adjutant Generals Office, *Roster of Wisconsin Volunteers, War of Rebellion, 1861-1865* (1886); Passenger Lists of Vessels Arriving at New York, 1820-1897 (National Archives Microfilm Publication M237, Roll M237_57); Index to New England Naturalization Petitions, 1791-1906 (National Archives and Records Administration, M1299, Microfilm Roll 43); Register of Enlistments in the US Army 1798-1914 (National Archives Microfilm Publication M233).

33 Official Records of the Union and Confederate Armies Series 1, Vol. 2, p. 369, 372.

34 *New York Irish American*, 9 September 1862, 'A Man Wounded Six Times in One Battle'.

35 Official Records Series 1, Vol. 2, p. 394; Walter F. Beyer and Oscar F. Keydel, *Deeds of Valor: How America's Heroes Won the Medal of Honor*, Vol. 1 (The Perrien-Keydel Company, 1901).

36 *New York Irish American*, 9 September 1862.

37 *New York Times*, 20 August 1861, 'The Monster Festival; Aid for the Widows and Orphans of the Sixty-Ninth Regiment'.

38 R.J. Proft, *United States of America's Congressional Medal of Honor Recipients and their Official Citations* (Highland House II, 2002), p. 934.

39 For detailed discussion of Irish motivations to join the Union Army and Irish views towards the war see Ural Bruce, *The Harp and the Eagle*; William L. Burton, *Melting Pot Soldiers: The Union's Ethnic Regiments* (Fordham University Press, 1998); Joseph Hernon Junior, *Celts, Catholics and Copperheads: Ireland Views the American Civil War* (Ohio State University Press, 1968).

40 *New York Irish American*, 5 October 1861.

41 *Ibid*.

42 *New York Times*, 3 October 1854; *New York Herald*, 7 October 1861; *New York Irish American*, 12 October 1861.

43 *New York Herald*, 7 October 1861.

44 Among the papers that carried extracts of Meagher's speech at the Academy were the *New York Times* which ran a piece on the event on 7 October 1861. The most complete account, from which the quotes in this chapter are drawn, appeared in the *New York Irish American* of 12 October 1861.

45 Roger D. Hunt & Jack R. Brown, *Brevet Brigadier Generals in Blue* (Olde Soldier Books, 1990), p.437; Harold F. Smith, 'Mulligan and the Irish Brigade' in *Journal of the Illinois State Historical Society* Vol. 56, No. 2, Summer 1963 (Authority of State of Illinois, 1963), pp.164–76.

46 Thomas G. Rodgers, *Irish-American Units in the Civil War* (Osprey Publishing 2008), p.6.

47 Smith, 'Mulligan and the Irish Brigade', pp.164–76.

48 Smith, 'Mulligan and the Irish Brigade'; Illinois Adjutant General's Report, Regimental and Unit Histories, 1861–1866, http://www.

illinoiscivilwar150.org/pdfs/RegimentHistAdjGenRpt.pdf (Accessed 3 October 2012).

49 Proft, *America's Congressional Medal of Honor Recipients*, p.835, 888.

50 Analysis has yet to be undertaken where the changing nature of the Irish component of the regiment through the war is considered. This could be achieved through an assessment of the enlistment dates of each of the soldiers in the unit.

51 All nativity information was collated by analysing each soldier in the 23rd Illinois's record on the Illinois Civil War Muster and Descriptive Rolls Database at http://www.ilsos.gov/isaveterans/ civilmustersrch.jsp (Accessed 1 December 2011). This information was then entered into an excel database to enable analysis of nativity data. The original research was presented at http://www. irishamericancivilwar, Damian Shiels, 'Where were 'Irish' Soldiers From? A Case Study of the 23rd Illinois Infantry' and Damian Shiels, 'Following Them Home: Discovering the Birthplaces of Irish Soldiers in the 23rd Illinois Infantry.' Analysis did not include Field Officers. Efforts were made to avoid duplication of individuals due to contemporary spelling discrepancies and multiple records, though some margin of error is unavoidable.

52 The 682 men recorded as of Irish birth account for 43 per cent of the total number of men for the regiment, 1,585. 315 men or 19.9 per cent of the men have no recorded place of birth. If these are excluded from the calculations, the Irish–born account for 53.85 of the remaining total. The 407 US born men account for 25.7 per cent of the total number of 1,585 soldiers.

53 The figures of confirmed Irish birth by company were: Company A: 51, Company B: 107, Company C: 62, Company D: 11, Company E: 28, Company F: 126, Company G: 76, Company H: 73, Company I: 61, Company K: 87.

54   Although the counties with the highest representations in the 23rd Illinois did suffer badly in Famine, other counties that also suffered high rates of emigration do not have a proportionate representation in the ranks.

55   The full nativity figures for the 23rd Illinois are: Ireland 682, United States 407, Unknown 315, England 47, Germany 42, Canada 39, Scotland 21, France 15, Norway 5, Sweden 3, Switzerland 3, Born at Sea 2, Netherlands 2, Wales 2.

56   James B. Swan and Damian Shiels, 'Where were Irish Soldiers From? A Case Study of the 90th Illinois Infantry' at http://irishamericancivilwar.com/2012/03/27/where-were-irish-soldiers-from-a-case-study-of-the-90th-illinois-infantry/ (Accessed 3 October 2012). I am grateful to James Swan for making the data on which that article is based available. 65.7% of the total number of enlisted men in the 90th Illinois were Irish, this figure increases to 69.6% when those men with no record place of birth are excluded. It forms a part of his history of the regiment: James B. Swan, *Chicago's Irish Legion: The 90th Illinois Volunteers in the Civil War* (Southern Illinois University Press, 2009).

57   For more on the human cost of the largest battles of the Civil War see the Civil War Trust Battles of the Civil War Infographic at http://www.civilwar.org/resources/battles-of-the-civil-war-infographic.html.

58   Roger D. Hunt, *Colonels in Blue: Union Army Colonels of the Civil War: New York* (Schiffer Military History, 2003), p.67; Bruce S. Allardice, *Confederate Colonels* (University of Missouri Press, 2008), p.360; Ural Bruce, *The Harp and the Eagle*, p. 13; David T. Gleeson, *The Irish in the South 1815-1877* (The University of North Carolina Press, 2001), p.27.

59   Rufus W. Clark, *The Heroes of Albany* (S.R. Gray, 1867), pp.236-7; Frederick Phisterer, *New York in the War of Rebellion 1861 to 1865*, Vol. 1 (J.B. Lyon Company, 1912) ; Franklin B. Hough, *History of*

Duryée s Brigade During the Campaign in Virginia under General Pope and in Maryland under General McClellan in the Summer and Autumn of 1862 (J. Munsell, Albany, 1864), p.43; James P. Gannon, *Irish Rebels, Confederate Tigers: A History of the 6th Louisiana Volunteers, 1861-1865* (Savas Publishing Company, 1998), p.328, 335.

60   Stephen W. Sears, *Landscape Turned Red: The Battle of Antietam* (Mariner Books, 2003), pp.185-7; Clark, *Heroes of Albany*, p.236.

61   Official Records Vol.19, Part 1, *Report of Brigadier-General Harry T. Hays, 1st Louisiana Brigade*, pp.978-9; Gannon, *Irish Rebels*, pp.132-9.

62   Gannon, *Irish Rebels*, pp.136-7.

63   Clark, *Heroes of Albany*, pp.238-9.

64   Alpheus S. Williams, *From The Cannon's* Mouth (University of Nebraska Press, 1995), p. 130; William A. Frassanito, *Antietam: The Photographic Legacy of America's Bloodiest Day* (Scribners, 1978), pp.122-5.

65   Hunt, *Colonels in Blue*, p.67; Oden Bowie, *A Descriptive List of the Burial Places of the Remains of Confederate Soldiers, Who Fell in the Battles of Antietam, South Mountain, Monocacy and Other Points in Washington and Frederick Counties, in the State of Maryland* (Free Press, Hagerstown, 1868), p.26.

66   For more on the New York Irish Colonels and Confederate Irish Colonels see Hunt, *Colonels in Blue* and Allardice, *Confederate Colonels*.

67   Christian G. Samito (ed.), 'Introduction' in Daniel George MacNamara, *The History of the Ninth Regiment, Massachusetts Volunteer Infantry* (Fordham University Press, 2000), pp.xi-xxxviii.

68   MacNamara, *The History of the Ninth Regiment*, pp.128-31; Christian G. Samito (ed.) *Commanding Boston's Irish Ninth: The Civil War Letters of Colonel Patrick R. Guiney, Ninth Massachusetts Volunteer Infantry* (Fordham University Press, 1998), p.115. See

also Michael H. MacNamara, *The Irish Ninth in Bivouac and Battle* (Lee and Shepard, 1867), pp.93-104.

69 For the best analysis of the battle see Gordon C. Rhea, *The Battle of the Wilderness, May 5-6, 1864* (Louisiana State University Press, 1994).

70 Samito (ed.), *Commanding Boston's Irish Ninth*, pp. 243-245; Rhea, *The Battle of the Wilderness*, pp. 145-208.

71 Rhea, *The Battle of the Wilderness*, p.102.

72 *Ibid.*, pp.145-70.

73 MacNamara, *The History of the Ninth Regiment*, p.372; Rhea, *The Battle of the Wilderness*, pp.169-70.

74 MacNamara, *The History of the Ninth Regiment*, p.372.

75 *Ibid.*

76 *Ibid*, p.373.

77 *Ibid*, pp.376-7.

78 Proft *America's Congressional Medal of Honor Recipients*, pp.1-5; Robert P. Broadwater, *Civil War Medal of Honor Recipients: A Complete Illustrated Record* (McFarland & Company, 2007), pp.4-6.

79 The most complete list of Irish-born Medal of Honor recipients has been compiled by the author and is available at http://irishamericancivilwar.com/resources/medal-of-honor-5/. The total number of Medal of Honor recipients from the Civil War was 1,527, breaking down as 1,200 to the army and 327 to the navy (See Broadwater, *Civil War Medal of Honor Recipients*, p.6). The Irish-born recipients constitute 9.6 per cent of this figure.

80 1860 Federal Census; *Worcester Daily Spy* 21 April 1896, 'Francis Plunkett'; Charles F. Walcott, *History of the 21st Regiment, Massachusetts Volunteers, in the War for Preservation of the Union, 1861-1865* (Houghton, Mifflin and Company, 1882), p.3, pp.174-5.

81 Francis Augustín O Reilly, *The Fredericksburg Campaign: Winter War on the Rappahannock* (Louisiana State University Press, 2003), p.337; Walcott, *History of the 21st Regiment*, p.241.

82   O'Reilly, *The Fredericksburg Campaign*, p.338; Walcott, *History of the 21st Regiment*, p.241; *New York Times*, 11 March 1885, 'Heroic Color Bearer Dead'.

83   Walcott, *History of the 21st Regiment*, p.241; *New York Times* 'Heroic Color Bearer Dead; O'Reilly, The Fredericksburg Campaign', p.340; Stephen B. Oates, *A Woman of Valor: Clara Barton and the Civil War* (The Free Press, 1994), p. 113.

84   Oates, *A Woman of Valor*, p.114

85   Walcott, *History of the 21st Regiment*, p.258.

86   Oates, *A Woman of Valor*, p.122

87   *Springfield Republican*, 1 April 1863, 'Miscellaneous War News'; *Boston Journal*, 10 March 1885, 'Obituary: Sergeant Thomas Plunkett'; *New York Times*, 'Heroic Color Bearer Dead'.

88   *Boston Journal* 'Obituary: Sergeant Thomas Plunkett'; Walcott, *History of the 21st Regiment*, p.304.

89   Broadwater, *Civil War Medal of Honor Recipients*, p.159; *Boston Journal*, 'Obituary: Sergeant Thomas Plunkett'; *Worcester Daily Spy*, 23 November 1895, 'Sergeant Thomas Plunkett's Portrait in Mechanics Hall'.

90   Proft (ed.), *Congressional Medal of Honor Recipients*, p.965.

91   Irving Ashby Buck, *Cleburne and His Command* (McCowat-Mercer Press, 1959), p.290-1. Irving Buck spent much of the war as Patrick Cleburne's adjutant.

92   Mauriel Phillips Joslyn, 'Irish Beginnings' in Mauriel Phillips Joslyn (ed.) *A Meteor Shining Brightly: Essays on Major-General Patrick R. Cleburne* (Mercer University Press, 2000), pp.1-17. See also Craig L. Symonds, *Stonewall of the West, Patrick Cleburne and the Civil War* (University Press of Kansas, 1997), particularly pp.9-25 and Bruce H. Stewart, Jr, *Invisible Hero: Patrick R. Cleburne* (Mercer University Press, 2009), particularly pp. 1-3.

93   Joslyn, 'Irish Beginnings'.

94   *Ibid.*

95   Symonds, *Stonewall of the West*, pp.45-63. For Cleburne's wartime career see also Joslyn (ed.), *A Meteor Shining Brightly* and Stewart Jr. *Invisible Hero*. The latter title focuses specifically on Cleburne's military career.

96   Buck, *Cleburne and his Command*, p. 195.

97   Eric A. Jacobsen & Richard A. Rupp, *For Cause and For Country: A Study of the Affair at Spring Hill and the Battle of Franklin* (O'More Publishing 2006), p.440.

98   Buck, *Cleburne and his Command*, p.291.

99   Buck, *Cleburne and his Command*, pp.291-2; Charles Frazer, 'Fifth Confederate' in John Berrien Lindsley (ed.), *The Military Annals of Tennessee: Confederate* (Lindsley & Co. Publishers, 1886), pp.146-54.

100 Buck, *Cleburne and his Command*, p. 293.

101 Buck, *Cleburne and his Command*, p. 280; Mauriel Phillips Joslyn, 'Epilogue' in Joslyn, *A Meteor Shining* Brightly, pp.183-92.

102 William J. Hardee, 'Biographical Sketch of Major General Patrick R. Cleburne' in John Francis Maguire, *The Irish in America* (D. & J. Sadlier & Co., 1868), pp.642-53; Thomas Y. Cartwright 'Franklin: The Valley of Death' in Mauriel Phillips Joslyn *A Meteor Shining Brightly*, pp.172-82.

103 *Philadelphia Inquirer*, 12 July 1865, 'Tribute to General Smyth'.

104 D.W. Maull, *The Life and Military Services of the Late Brigadier General Thomas A. Smyth* (H. & E.F. James, 1870), p.6; New York Passenger Lists, 1820-1957, Thomas was listed on the *Sardinia* under the spelling 'Smith'.

105 David Power Conyngham, *The Irish Brigade and its Campaigns* (William McSorley & Co. 1867), p.541; Maull, *The Life and Military Services*, pp.6-7.

106 *Ibid.*, pp.7-8.

107 Maull, *The Life and Military Services*, pp.9-16; Stephen W. Sears, *Gettysburg* (Mariner Books, 2004), p.404, 410.

108 Conyngham, *The Irish Brigade*, p.542; Maull, *The Life and Military Services*, p.18.

109 Maull, *The Life and Military Services*, p.19.

110 Warner, *Generals in Blue*, p.466; Maull, *The Life and Military Services*, pp.35–8.

111 *New York Irish American Weekly*, 25 February 1865, 'Fenian Brotherhood: Official Minutes of the Central Council of the Fenian Brotherhood, February 9, 1865'; *New York Irish American Weekly*, 22 April 1865, 'Death of Gen. Thomas A. Smyth'; Michael H. Kane, 'American Soldiers in Ireland, 1865–67', in Kenneth Ferguson (ed.), *The Irish Sword: Journal of the Military History Society of Ireland*, Vol. 23, No. 91, Summer 2002, pp.103–40.

112 Noah Andre Trudeau, *The Last Citadel: Petersburg, Virginia, June 1864-April 1865* (Little, Brown 1991), pp.355–423.

113 Maull, *The Life and Military Services*, pp.42–3.

114 *Ibid.*, p.41.

115 *Ibid.*, p.43.

116 Maull, *The Life and Military Services*, pp.43–5; *Philadelphia Inquirer*, 15 April 1865, 'The Funeral of General Smyth'.

117 J. David Hacker, 'Recounting the Dead', *New York Times*, 20 September 2011; http://opinionator.blogs.nytimes.com/2011/09/20/recounting-the-dead/ (Accessed 20 September 2012). Hacker's research, centring on census analysis, suggests the long-held figure of 620,000 soldier deaths is inaccurate. His work indicates the real figure to be between 750,000 and 850,000; Drew Gilpin Faust, *This Republic of Suffering: Death and the American Civil War* (Alfred A. Knopf, 2008), pp.xi-xii, 273–4. Although no figures have been compiled for civilian deaths in the war, Faust cites James McPherson with regard to the estimate of 50,000 civilian deaths. McPherson, *Battle Cry of Freedom*, p.796.

118 Samuel Penniman Bates, *History of Pennsylvania Volunteers 1861-5*, Vol. 3 (B. Singerly 1870), p.1,267, 1,306; Frank Hamilton Taylor,

Philadelphia in the Civil War 1861-1865 (City of Philadelphia, 1913) p.172; Ancient Order of Hibernians Bristol Division, 'Michael Dougherty', http://www.aohbristol.com/HomePage.htm (Accessed 20 September 2012).

119   Michael Dougherty, *Prison Diary, of Michael Dougherty, Late Co. B, 13th., Pa., Cavalry. While Confined in Pemberton, Barrett's, Libby, Andersonville and Other Southern Prisons* (Chas. A. Dougherty, 1908), pp. i–ii, 1.

120   Taylor, *Philadelphia in the Civil War*, p.172; Bates, *History of Pennsylvania Volunteers*, p.1,269; Dougherty, *Prison Diary*, p.72.

121   Dougherty, *Prison Diary*, pp.14–17.

122   *Ibid.*, pp.18–19.

123   *Ibid.*, p.20.

124   *Ibid.*, p.21.

125   *Ibid.*, p.27.

126   *Ibid.*, p.40.

127   *Ibid.*, p.43.

128   *Ibid.*, p.44.

129   *Ibid.*, p.54.

130   For a history of the 10th Tennessee Infantry see Ed Gleeson, *Rebel Sons of Erin* (Guild Press of Indiana, 1993). Dougherty, *Prison Diary*, p.40, 43, 54, 65.

131   Dougherty, *Prison Diary*, pp.68–71.

132   Dougherty, *Prison Diary*, p.71; Ancient Order of Hibernians Bristol Division, 'Michael Dougherty'; Proft, *America's Congressional Medal of Honor Recipients*, p. 847.

133   David Power Conyngham, *The Irish Brigade*, pp.5–6. For the best discussion of why the Union was so important to those in the North, see Gary W. Gallagher, *The Union War* (Harvard University Press, 2011).

134   Ural Bruce, *The Harp and the Eagle*, pp.112–13, 119–23. There were a number of other factors that led to the drop off in Irish support

for the war and their antipathy towards the black community. For a detailed analysis see Ural Bruce, *The Harp and the Eagle.*

135   Iver Bernstein, *The New York City Draft Riots: Their Significance for American Society and Politics in the Age of the Civil War* (Oxford University Press, 1990), pp.7–11.

136   Ural Bruce, *The Harp and the Eagle*, p.180; Roger D. Hunt & Jack R. Brown, *Brevet Brigadier Generals in Blue,* (Olde Soldier Books, 199), p.451.

137   Roger D. Hunt, *Colonels in Blue*, p.214; 3rd Annual Report of the Bureau of Military Statistics, '11th Regiment New York Volunteer Infantry' http://dmna.ny.gov/historic/reghist/civil/infantry/11thInf/11thInfBMSHistSketch.htm accessed 21 September 2012.

138   *New York Times*, 15 July 1863, 'The Riot in Second Avenue'; David M. Barnes, *The Draft Riots in New York, July 1863: The Service of the Metropolitan Police* (Baker & Godwin, 1868), p.37.

139   *New York Times*, 15 July 1863; Barnes, *The Draft Riots in New York*, p.37; New York State Military Museum 11th New York Newspaper Clippings, http://dmna.ny.gov/historic/reghist/civil/infantry/11thInf/11thInfCWN.htm (Accessed 21 September 2012).

140   11th New York Newspaper Clippings.

141   11th New York Newspaper Clippings; *Harper's Weekly*, 1 August 1863, 'The Riots at New York'.

142   *New York Herald*, 9 August 1863, 'The Murder of Colonel O'Brien'; *New York Times*, 4 July 1867, 'The Murder of Col. O'Brien: Arrest of the Alleged Murderer'.

143   *New York Herald*, 30 January 1864, 'The Late Colonel O'Brien'.

144   Hunt, *Colonels in Blue*, p.214.

145   Ural Bruce, *The Harp and the Eagle*, p.13; McPherson, *Battle Cry of Freedom*, pp.609–10.

146   Lawrence Frederick Kohl with Margaret Cossé Richard (eds.), *Irish Green and Union Blue: The Civil War Letters of Peter Welsh* (Fordham University Press, 1986), p.110.

147 Ural Bruce, *The Harp and the Eagle*, p.189.

148 *New York Herald*, 13 May 1863, 'Reported Recruitment of British Subjects'.

149 Ella Lonn, *Foreigners in the Confederacy* (The University of North Carolina Press, 2002), pp.74-5.

150 Civil War Service Record of J.L. Capston; *Southern Historical Society Papers*, Vol. 24, 'Special Mission of Lieut. J.L. Capston to Ireland', pp.202-4.

151 *Ibid*.

152 Lonn, *Foreigners in the Confederacy*, pp.76-7.

153 Lonn, *Foreigners in the Confederacy*, pp.75-7; Official Records of the Union and Confederate Navies in the War of Rebellion Series 2, Vol. 3, pp. 893-895. Father Bannon has been the subject of two biographies, Phillip Thomas Tucker, *The Confederacy's Fighting Chaplain: Father John B. Bannon* (University of Alabama Press, 1992) and William Barnaby Faherty S.J., *Exile in Erin, A Confederate Chaplain's Story: The Life of Father John B. Bannon* (Missouri History Museum Press, 2002).

154 Official Records, pp.893-5; Lonn, *Foreigners in the Confederacy*, pp.77-9.

155 *Edinburgh Gazette*, 17 August 1855, 'Commissions'; Felix Gregory De Fontaine, *Marginalia, or, Gleanings from an Army Notebook* (F.G. DeFontaine & Co., 1864), p.99.

156 De Fontaine, *Marginalia*, p.99.

157 Civil War Service Record of Robert Going Atkins; *Atlanta Daily Constitutionalist*, 13 April 1864, 'Enlistments in Ireland'.

158 *Richmond Examiner*, 3 December 1864, 'Death of a Gallant Gentleman'.

159 *New York Irish American*, 19 February 1870, 'Munster'.

160 Amanda Foreman, *A World On Fire: An Epic History of Two Nations Divided* (Allen Lane, 2010), p.583.

161 Lonn, *Foreigners in the Confederacy*, p.79. Lonn cites two sources for Irish immigration figures, Sir Robert Peel, Secretary for Ireland, who put the figure at 117,000 in 1863 and 114,000 in 1864, and the report of the United States commissioner for immigration who listed 55,916 for 1863 and 63,523 in 1864.

162 William Marvel, *The Alabama and the Kearsarge: The Sailor's Civil War* (University of North Carolina Press, 1996), p.202.

163 Marvel, *The Alabama and the Kearsarge*, p.202-3; Official Records of the Union and Confederate Navies in the War of Rebellion Series 1, Vol. 2, p.489.

164 Marvel, *The Alabama and the Kearsarge*, p.203; Enlistment of British Seamen at Queenstown; British Parliamentary Papers, 1864, LXII [168], pp.209-21, http://ied.dippam.ac.uk/records/20927 (Accessed 22 September 2012). Enlistment of Emigrants in the US Navy; British Parliamentary Papers, 1864, LXII, (203), pp. 369-377, http://ied.dippam.ac.uk/records/39897 (Accessed 22 September 2012).

165 Enlistment of British Seamen at Queenstown.

166 Marvel, *The Alabama and the Kearsarge*, pp.204-5; Official Records, p.563; Enlistment of British Seaman at Queenstown; Scott Reynolds Nelson & Carol Sheriff, *A People at War: Civilians and Soldiers in America's Civil War* (Oxford University Press, 2008), pp. 169-71.

167 Enlistment of British Seaman at Queenstown; Nelson & Sheriff, *A People at War*, pp.169-71. Nelson and Sheriff present a convincing argument that Kennedy and Lynch had no reason to know the consul, and that they may have been put up to their statements by Confederate agents. Adams believed this to be the case, saying the ship's captain had fallen into a trap.

168 Marvel, *The Alabama and the Kearsarge*, pp.203-4; Official Records, p.565; Debate on the *Kearsarge* Federal Enlistments in

Ireland; Hansard Parliamentary Debates, Series 3, Vol. 174, March 18 1864, http://ied.dippam.ac.uk/records/35034 (Accessed 22 September 2012).

169   Marvel, *The Alabama and the Kearsarge*, pp.204-5; Official Records, p.563; pp.124-37; John M. Ellicot, *The Life of John Ancrum Winslow, Rear-Admiral, United States Navy* (The Knickerbocker Press, 1901), p.129; Debate on the *Kearsarge* Federal Enlistments In Ireland.

170   Nelson & Sheriff, *A People at War*, pp. 170-1; Enlistment of Emigrants in the US Navy.

171   Marvel, *The Alabama and the Kearsarge*, pp.204-5; Enlistment of British Seaman at Queenstown.

172   Marvel, *The Alabama and the Kearsarge*, pp.248-54.

173   Proft, *America's Congressional Medal of Honor Recipients*, p. 786.

174   *New York Times*, 20 October 1862, 'Brady's Photographs; Pictures of the Dead at Antietam'.

175   *Time Magazine*, 17 February 1961, 'Artist-Journalists of the Civil War'.

176   *New York Times*, 18 September 1912, 'Arthur Lumley Artist Dies'; Sheila Gallagher, Arthur Lumley 1837-1912', http://idesweb. bc.edu/becker/artists/lumley (Accessed 22 September 2012).

177   *New York Times*, 'Arthur Lumley Artist Dies'; Sheila Gallagher, *Arthur Lumley*.

178   Alpheus S. Williams, *From the Cannon's Mouth*, p.180.

179   James D. Horan, *Timothy O'Sullivan: America's Forgotten Photographer* (Bonanza Books, 1966), pp.22-34. Although in one job application Timothy listed his birth place as New York, his father listed it as Ireland on his 1882 birth certificate. It may be that Timothy lied on the application in an attempt to avoid anti-Irish prejudice.

180   Horan, *Timothy O'Sullivan*, pp.31-5.

181   Horan, *Timothy O'Sullivan*, pp.3-4, 34.

182 Horan, *Timothy O'Sullivan*, pp.44-5; William A. Frassanito, *Gettysburg: A Journey in Time* (Thomas Publications, 1975), pp.190-2, 228-9.

183 Horan, *Timothy O'Sullivan*, pp.46-53.

184 *New York Times*, 'Arthur Lumley Artist Dies'; Sheila Gallagher, *Arthur Lumley*; *Lumley*; Horan, *Timothy O'Sullivan*, pp.151-312.

185 *New York Times*, 'Arthur Lumley Artist Dies'; Sheila Gallagher, *Arthur Lumley*; *New York Herald Tribune*, 7 November 1890, 'For the Benefit of Arthur Lumley'; Horan, *Timothy O'Sullivan*, pp.313-18.

186 Illinois Civil War Muster and Descriptive Rolls Database, http://www.ilsos.gov/isaveterans/civilmustersrch.jsp (Accessed 24 September 2012); Wales W. Woods, *A History of the Ninety-Fifth Regiment Illinois Infantry Volunteers* (Tribune Company's Book and Job Printing Office, 1865) p.226; Lon P. Dawson, *Also Known as Albert D.J. Cashier: The Jennie Hodgers Story, or How One Young Irish Girl Joined the Union Army During the Civil War* (Illinois Veteran's Home, 2005), pp.25-6.

187 Dawson, *Also Known*, p.5; Salt Magazine, *What Part am I to Act in this Great Drama: Women Soldiers in the American Civil War*, http://www.saltmag.net/givetous/Andrea_21405.pdf (Accessed 17 August 2011); Rodney O. Davis, 'Private Albert Cashier as Regarded by His/Her Comrades', *Illinois Historical Journal* 82 (1989), pp.108-12.

188 Deposition of J.H. Himes 24 January 1915, http://www.archives.gov/publications/prologue/images/women-soldiers-deposition.jpg (Accessed 24 September 2012).

189 'Remarkable War Veteran: Woman Fought Three Years in Civil War', *The Hartford Republican*, 6 June 1913.

190 Davis, 'Private Albert Cashier', pp.110-12.

191 Davis, 'Private Albert Cashier', p.108; 'Remarkable War Veteran: Woman Fought Three Years in Civil War', *The Hartford Republican*.

192 Gerhard P. Clausius, 'The Little Soldier of the 95th: Albert D.J. Cashier', *Illinois Historical Journal* 51 (1958), pp.380-7. Albert D.J. Cashier Civil War Pension Index Card.

193 Clausius, 'The Little Soldier of the 95th' pp.385-6; Davis, 'Private Albert Cashier', p. 109; *The Democratic Banner*, 6 May 1913, 'Masqueraded as Man for Over 50 Years: Remarkable Career of Woman Inmate of Soldiers' Home'.

194 'Remarkable War Veteran: Woman Fought Three Years in Civil War', *The Hartford Republican*

195 *Ibid*.

196 Clausius, 'The Little Soldier of the 95th', p.386; Davis, 'Private Albert Cashier', p.110.

197 Clausius, 'The Little Soldier of the 95th', p.387.

198 WBEZ91.5, *Jennie's House: Part of a Civil War Secret*, http://www.wbez.org/story/jennies-house-preserving-part-civil-war-secret-91446 (Accessed 24 September 2012). I am grateful to Andy Hall of www.deadconfederates.com for bringing the restoration of this house to my attention.

199 William Watt Hart Davis, *History of the 104th Pennsylvania Regiment from August 22nd 1861 to September 30th 1864* (Jas. B. Rodgers, 1866), p.123.

200 Charles A. Hale, *My Personal Experiences at the Battle of Antietam*, John Rutter Brooke Papers, Historical Society of Pennsylvania. I am grateful to Irish Brigade researcher Robert McLernon for bringing this account to my attention.

201 *Oregonian*, 4 June 1911, 'Heroic Women at the Cannons Mouth in the Civil War'. Bridget's surname is variously spelt Diver(s), Deaver(s) and Devens in the historical record.

202 Richard Hall, *Patriots in Disguise: Women Warrior's of the Civil War* (Paragon House, 1993), p.28; Frank Moore, *Women of the War;*

Their Heroism and Self-Sacrifice (S.S. Scranton & Co., 1867), p.109.

203 Mary A. Livermore, *My Story of the War: A Woman's Narrative of Four Years Personal Experience* (A.D. Worthington & Company, 1889), pp.116–19.

204 Charlotte E. McKay, *Stories of Hospital and Camp* (Claxton, Remsen & Haffelfinger 1876), p.125.

205 Moore, *Women of the War,* pp.461–2.

206 Moore, *Women of the War,* pp.109–12; *Washington Evening Star,* 21 September 1892, 'Irish Biddy'.

207 'Miss Mary S. Hill' in *Confederate Veteran,* Vol. 10, March 1902, p.124; Mary Sophia Hill, *A British Subject's Recollections of the Confederacy while a Visitor and Attendant in it's Hospitals and Camps* (Turnbull Brothers 1875) transcribed by Jan Batte Craven for the Louisiana Division, United Daughters of the Confederacy, http://www.rootsweb.ancestry.com/~laudc/maryhilldiary.html (Accessed 22 September 2012). For a history of the 6th Louisana see James P. Gannon, *Irish Rebels, Confederate Tigers: A History of the 6th Louisiana Volunteers, 1861-1865* (Savas Publishing Company, 1998).

208 Hill, *A British Subject's Recollections,* p.10.

209 *Ibid.,* pp.19–20.

210 *Ibid.,* pp.61–111.

211 *Ibid.,* p.61.

212 *Confederate Veteran,* p.124.

213 *Ibid.*

214 David Power Conyngham, *The Irish Brigade,* p.129.

215 *Ibid.*

216 Annual Report of the Adjutant-General for the State of New York for the Year 1901 (J.B. Lyon & Co., 1902), p.50; Patrick Casey Widow's Pension File (WC13081).

217 Patrick Casey Widow's Pension File.

218 Ibid.

219 Obituary – Lieutenant Patrick Henry Hayes, Thirty-Seventh
Regiment New York Volunteers, New York State Military
Museum, http://dmna.ny.gov/historic/reghist/civil/
infantry/37thInf/37thInfCWN.htm (Accessed 25 September 2012).

220 *New York Irish American*, 24 May 1862, '37th N.Y.V., "Irish Rifles"';
Patrick Henry Hayes Widow's Pension File (WC3561); Michael H.
Kane, 'American Soldiers in Ireland 1865-67' in *The Irish Sword:
The Journal of the Military History Society of Ireland*, Vol.23, No.91,
Summer 2002, pp.103-40.

221 *Irish American*, '37th N.Y.V.'.

222 Patrick Henry Hayes Widow's Pension File.

223 Patrick Henry Hayes Widow's Pension File. Bridget had been
present at the baptism of Ellen, which suggests she had known
Dorcas for some years.

224 1880 Federal Census, Patrick Henry Hayes Widow's Pension File.

225 Ibid.

226 Ibid.

227 Proft, *America's Congressional Medal of Honor Recipients*, p. 850;
Robert P. Broadwater, *Civil War Medal of Honor Recipients: A
Complete Illustrated Record* (McFarland & Company, 2007), p.67.
Richard Dunphy's year of birth is variously recorded as both 1840
and 1842.

228 Navy Widow's Certificates, Richard D. Dunphy, File No. 17218.

229 Ibid.

230 Ibid.

231 Ibid.

232 Ibid.

233 Ibid.

234 National Park Service, *History of the National Home for Disabled
Volunteer Soldiers*, http://www.nps.gov/nr/travel/veterans_affairs/
History.html (Accessed 3 October 2012).

235 US National Home for Disabled Volunteer Soldiers 1866–1938, James Manning entries for Mountain Branch, North-western Branch, Central Branch, Eastern Branch, Western Branch, Bath Branch and Roseburg Branch; James Manning Pension Index Card (Application No. 82986, Certificate No. 75501).

236 *List of Pensioners on the Roll, January 1, 1883*, Volume 5 (Washington Government Printing Office, 1883), p. 638; Peter Keefe Navy Survivor Certificate No. 843.

237 *List of Pensioners on the Roll*, pp. 638–9; *Annual Report of Adjutant General of the State of New York for the Year 1899*, (James B. Lyon Printers, 1900), p.839, 956. Louis Wilson Civil War Pension Index Card, Certificate No. 52.311; George Church Civil War Pension Index Card, Certificate No. 43,673.

238 James L. Swanson, *Manhunt: The 12-Day Chase for Abraham Lincoln's Killer* (Portrait, 2006), pp.32–48.

239 John Franklin Sprague, *New York, The Metropolis: It's Noted Professional and Business Men* (The New York Recorder, 1893), p.73; James Rowan O'Beirne US Passport Application 25 October 1889; *New York Times*, 18 February 1917, 'Gen. Jas. R. O'Beirne Dies in 77th Year'; *Philadelphia Inquirer*, 19 February 1917, 'Obituary: Gen. James R. O'Beirne'; James Rowan O'Beirne's date of birth is variously given as 1838, 1840 and 1842. His obituaries do not agree on his age, some listing him as seventy-seven and some as seventy-five at the time of his death. O'Beirne himself listed his date of birth as 1842 on an 1889 Passport Application, and this date has been followed here.

240 Swanson, *Manhunt*, pp.90–4; *Macon Telegraph*, 30 June 1889, 'An Incident of History: James R. O'Beirne Corrects A Statement Regarding Lincoln's Death'.

241 *Macon Telegraph*, 'An Incident of History'; Swanson, *Manhunt*, pp.52–61, 78–9.

242 Swanson, *Manhunt* pp.138–139; *Macon Telegraph*, 'An Incident of History'.

243 *New York Times*, 7 December 1930, 'A New Version of the Greatest Man Hunt: Major O'Beirne's Diary, Recently Brought to Light, Describes the Difficulties of the Chase After Lincoln's Assassination'.

244 *Ibid*.

245 Swanson, *Manhunt* p.176; *New York Times*, 'A New Version'.

246 Osborn H. Oldroyd, *The Assassination of Abraham Lincoln: Flight, Pursuit, Capture and Punishment of the Conspirators* (O.H. Oldroyd, 1901), pp.66–8; *New York Times*, 'A New Version'.

247 Oldroyd, *The Assassination of Abraham Lincoln*, pp.67–8; *New York Times*, 'A New Version'.

248 Swanson, *Manhunt*, pp. 316–43, 190–3, 219–20, 364–6; Thomas Reed Turner, *Beware the People Weeping: Public Opinion and the Assassination of Abraham Lincoln* (Louisiana State University Press, 1982), pp.113–15. Turner outlines how Baker most probably viewed O'Beirne's messages to Stanton prior to making his decision on where to pursue Booth.

249 Turner, *Beware the People Weeping*, p.115.

250 Sprague, *New York, The Metropolis*, p.73; *New York Times*, 'Gen. Jas. R. O'Beirne Dies'; Roger D. Hunt & Jack R. Brown, *Brevet Brigadier Generals in Blue* (Olde Soldier Books, 199), p.453; Proft *America's Congressional Medal of Honor Recipients*, p. 952.

251 *New York Irish American*, 13 February 1909, 'At the Lincoln Memorial Meeting'; *New York Times*, 'Gen. Jas. R. O'Beirne Dies'; Hunt & Brown, *Brevet Brigadier Generals*, p.453.

252 Robert S. Lanier, *The Photographic History of the Civil War: Volume Ten: Armies and Leaders* (The Review of Reviews Co. 1911), pp. 288–9.

253   *Baltimore American*, 26 April 1911, 'Finds Brother After 47 Years: New Jersey Businessman Sees Long Lost Photograph Taken During the Civil War'.

254   *Annual Report of the Adjutant-General of the State of New York for the Year 1905* (J.B. Lyon & Co. 1905) p.423.

255   *New York Tribune*, 9 December 1912, 'Irish Brigade to Meet'.

256   *The Washington Herald*, 14 December 1912, 'Irish Veterans Hold Reunion'.

257   *New York Sun*, 15 December 1912, 'Veterans of Famous Irish Brigade Dined'.

258   *New York Tribune*, 'Irish Brigade to Meet'; *New York Sun*, 'Veterans of Famous Irish Brigade Dined'; *New York Irish*, American 21 December 1912, 'The Dinner in Honor of the Survivors'; *New York Irish American*, 21 December 1912, 'Survivors of the Irish Brigade Honored'.

259   *New York Sun*, 'Veterans of Famous Irish Brigade Dined'.

260   *New York Evening World*, 14 December 1912, 'Survivors of the Dashing Meagher's Brigade who Stormed Marye's Heights Fifty Years Ago'.

261   Jeremiah O'Brien Texas Confederate Pension File No. 50513.

262   *Ibid*.

263   *Dallas Morning News*, 29 June 1950, '3 Confederates Left in Texas as J.P. O'Brien Dies'.

264   *The Beaumont Enterprise*, 29 June 1950, 'Honored Veteran Passes'.

265   For a discussion of the Irish efforts to highlight their wartime contribution in the post-war North see Ural Bruce, *The Harp and the Eagle*, pp.257–262; also for post-war challenges facing the Irish see *ibid*, pp.263–4.

266   Anthony W. McDermott, *A Brief History of the 69th Regiment Pennsylvania Veteran Volunteers* (D.J. Gallagher & Co., 1889), pp.29–30; Stephen W. Sears, *Gettysburg* (Mariner Books, 2004),

pp.392-393. For a detailed account of the 69th at Gettysburg see Don Ernsberger, *At the Wall: The 69th Pennsylvania "Irish Volunteers" at Gettysburg* (Xlibris, 2006).

267 McDermott, *A Brief History of the 69th Regiment*, p.32; Frank A. Boyle, *A Party of Mad Fellows: The Story of the Irish Regiments in the Army of the Potomac* (Morningside, 1996), p. 289.

268 *Philadelphia Inquirer*, 17 June 1887, 'Going to Gettysburg: Meeting of the Philadelphia Brigade to Complete Arrangements for the Trip'.

269 McDermott, *A Brief History of the 69th Regiment*, p.53.

270 *Ibid.*, pp.68-9.

271 *Ibid.*, pp.69-70.

272 Ibid., pp.75-6.

273 *Ibid.*, pp.71-2.

274 Letitia Baldridge Hollensteiner, recorded interview by Mrs Wayne Fredericks, April 24 1964 (19), John F. Kennedy Library Oral History Program, JFKOH-LKB-01, http://www.jfklibrary.org/Asset-Viewer/Archives/JFKOH-LKB-01.aspx (Accessed 7 October 2012)

275 David Power Conyngham, *The Irish Brigade*, pp. 330-7, 354.

276 Papers of John F. Kennedy, Presidential Papers, President's Office Files, 'Address to the Irish Parliament, Dublin, 28 June 1963' John F. Kennedy Presidential Library and Museum, http://www.jfklibrary.org/Asset-Viewer/Archives/JFKPOF-045-036.aspx (Accessed 7 October 2012); JKF's scriptwriter had allowed a number of clear inaccuracies to slip into the final version of the speech; for example Fredericksburg was fought on the 13 December in Virginia, rather than 13 September in Maryland. One wonders if in an earlier draft Antietam (fought in September 1862 in Maryland) may have been chosen as the battle to focus on, and that when it was changed to Fredericksburg the details were only partially altered. The casualty figures given for the Brigade are also incorrect, and the new colors were not carried at Fredericksburg.

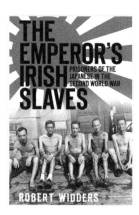
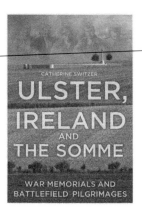